We've got... we've got *complicated*

Being the second collection of articles from the Parikiaki newspaper

James Neophytou

MAPLE
PUBLISHERS

We've got simple, we've got complicated

Author: James Neophytou

Copyright © James Neophytou (2023)

The right of James Neophytou to be identified as author of this work has been asserted by the author in accordance with section 77 and 78 of the Copyright, Designs and Patents Act 1988.

First Published in 2023

ISBN 978-1-915996-48-0 (Paperback)
      978-1-915996-49-7 (eBook)

Book cover and Book layout by:

    White Magic Studios
    www.whitemagicstudios.co.uk

Published by:

    Maple Publishers
    Fairbourne Drive, Atterbury,
    Milton Keynes,
    MK10 9RG, UK
    www.maplepublishers.com

A CIP catalogue record for this title is available from the British Library.

All rights reserved. No part of this book may be reproduced or translated by any form or by any means, electronic or mechanical, including photocopying, recording or by any information storage and retrieval system without written permission from the author.

The views expressed in this work are solely those of the author and do not necessarily reflect the views of the publisher, and the publisher hereby disclaims any responsibility for them.

'*Austerity* is the idea that the worldwide financial crash of 2008 was caused by Wolverhampton having too many libraries.'

– Alexei Sayle

'**George W. Bush:** I'm a war president. We're at war.

Colin Powell: Maybe because my whole life has been in the army I'm less impressed than some people by the use of force. I see it for what it is.

Bush: What is it?

Powell: Failure.

(Bush smiles).'

– David Hare, 'Stuff Happens'

For my parents

BY THE SAME AUTHOR

Angels of Morphia

Praise for *Angels of Morphia (2022)*

'Beautifully written.'
– *Maria Procopiou, lawyer*

'Loved reading it.'
– *John Northover, technology consultant*

'Fascinating. Informative. Great.'
– *Liam Fowler, risk analyst*

'Loving it.'
– *Tessa Coe, artist*

'Enjoyable and entertaining.'
– *Kevin Brankin, art teacher*

'There are a couple of good ones if you pick well.'
– *Bambos Neophytou, marketing consultant*

'Enjoyed it. Found lots of new ideas.'
– *Kanber Calibasi, maths teacher*

Contents

Introduction 9

I – Women 11
    1 Simone 12
    2 Simone II 15
    3 Shelagh 18
    4 Hermettes 21

II – Men 24
    5 Ayer 25
    6 Thomas 28
    7 Dennis 32
    8 Nuncle 35
    9 Hitch 39
    10 Women 42

III – Health 45
    11 Meat 46
    12 Now 49
    13 Stoic 52

IV – Culture 55
    14 Quiz 56
    15 Dragons 60

V – Music 63
    16 Biblical 64
    17 Morrissey 67
    18 Rollers 70

VI – Drama 74
- 19 Assassin 75
- 20 List 79
- 21 Patriots 83
- 22 Elvis 86
- 23 Antigone 89
- 24 Jeanne 92

VII – Technology 95
- 25 Quakes 96
- 26 Africa 99
- 27 Magic 102
- 28 Redesign 109

VIII – Work 112
- 29 Chile 113
- 30 Teaching IV 116
- 31 Teaching V 120
- 32 Cobalt 124

IX – Books 127
- 33 Salman 128
- 34 Boxer 131
- 35 Liz 134

X – Places 137
- 36 Jurisdictions 138
- 37 Iraq 141
- 38 Cyprus 144

XI – Society 148
- 39 Eichmann 149
- 40 Eichmann II 152
- 41 Eichmann III 155
- 42 Water 158

	43 Cult	161
	44 Fall	164
	45 Trickle	167
	46 Idealists	170
	47 Singapore	173
	48 Defeat	177

XII – Greeks 181
    49 Honey 182
    50 Secret 185

XIII – Language 188
    51 Jokes 189
    52 Italiano 192
    53 Speech 195
    54 Manc 199

XIV – Sport 202
    55 Klopp 203
    56 Philosophy 206
    57 Onanistic 209
    58 Physics 212

XV – Community 215
    59 Giuliani 216
    60 Light 219
    61 Lancashire 222
    62 Grounded 226
    63 Rules 230

Epilogue 233
Acknowledgements 234
References 235
Index 238

Introduction

Inside Robben Island prison, the only books allowed were holy ones.

Luckily, somebody managed to smuggle in the complete works of Shakespeare, disguised under a Bible cover.

Eventually, the prisoners read the plays and passed the book around. They signed it.

Movingly, when prisoner number *46664* signed the book, he added a quote from *Julius Caesar* next to his name:—

'Cowards die many times before their death,
The valiant never taste of death but once.'
                    ... Nelson Mandela

This book is the second collection of weekly articles that were published in the *English Section* of the *Parikiaki* newspaper.

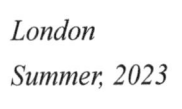

London
Summer, 2023

I – Women

'The band of the Scots Guards.'
> — *Her late Majesty Queen Elizabeth II, on being asked who played best at a football match she attended*

1 Simone

A modern saint of action

'She is the only great spirit of our times.'
– *Albert Camus*

Empathy

When she was six years old, Simone Weil refused to eat sugar, because it was not available to the soldiers on the front line of the First World War. This was a pattern of behaviour that she would repeat in her short, illuminating and inspiring life.

Born in 1909, to a comfortable Jewish family, she was one of the first women to enter the elite Paris university, *École Normale Supérieure*. Highly gifted, she studied Philosophy, but unlike her Parisian Left-Bank contemporaries, Weil *lived* and *breathed* her values and beliefs. Her fellow students would say that whenever they saw her she was would always ask them to sign some petition or other.

She lived an unfathomably full life, and died aged 34 in England, in 1943, from tuberculosis, cardiac failure and anorexia. Complications were caused by her insistence on eating only those rations allowed in occupied France during the *Second* World War.

She was one of the most influential writers of the twentieth century. President de Gaulle of France asked her to write a new French Constitution, in 1943. The result was a miraculous book called *The Need for Roots*, which everyone should read. General de Gaulle rejected it, considering it too spiritual and insufficiently secular. I say pish to General Charles de Gaulle – it's a remarkable, indispensable book.

Her actions and writing deeply influenced Simone de Beauvoir (her classmate), Jean-Paul Sartre, Albert Camus, Iris Murdoch, T.S. Eliot, Aleksandr Solzhenitsyn, Susan Sontag, Sir Roger Scruton, and several Popes. Her own influences were Plato, Descartes, Sophocles, Homer, Marx, Kierkegaard, and William Blake.

Social activism

After graduating, Weil taught philosophy in schools, and wrote articles for left-wing periodicals (*L'Humanité*, *Revue prolétarienne* and *École émancipée*), but she never belonged to any political party.

In 1932, she visited Germany to assist Marxist activists at a time of social crisis, high unemployment, and widespread despair among the youth. The situation seemed ripe for revolution, but she quickly saw that the communists were no match for the fascists. Returning home to France, Weil voiced her concerns to friends at what was taking shape in Germany – only to be dismissed. A year later Hitler came to power.

Later in her life, she regarded all political parties and trade unions as virtually totalitarian organisations that prevented their members from thinking for themselves.

Sublime bravery

Weil couldn't just watch from the sidelines. In 1934, she stopped teaching and applied to work in a Parisian car factory. Her first act was to ask for the payslips of the workers. She complained that they weren't paid enough.

Wanting to understand working-class lives, Weil observed that the workers became emotionless. The monotony of the work, and the constant scrutiny from management, led to their numb, slave-like state.

She wanted to walk in the shoes of the powerless. In 1936 Weil went to serve in the Spanish Civil War on the Republican side, and later assisted the French Resistance. Weil wasn't content to just theorise about the disenfranchised.

She spun the Cartesian motto ('I think, there I am') into one that was fit for the times, for an era that urgently needed action. She said, 'I *can*, therefore I am. I *will*, therefore I am.'

In the last years of her life, Weil turned towards Christianity. Following Aeschylus, she believed that knowledge was gained through suffering.

Throughout Simone Weil's life, her peerless moral courage set her apart. She went out into the field and practiced what she preached.

2 Simone II

The outsider's outsider

'She has a heart that could beat all over the world.'
– *Simone de Beauvoir*

Simone Weil (1909-43) belonged to a species so rare, it had only one member.

The French philosopher and mystic diagnosed the maladies of her own age and place – Europe in the first, war-torn, half of the 20th century – and offered recommendations for how to delay or halt the unfairness of totalitarianism, income inequality, restriction of free speech, political polarisation, and modern alienation.

Her combination of erudition, political and spiritual fervour, and commitment to her ideals adds weight to the unique diagnosis she offers of modernity. Weil has been dead now for 80 years but remains able to tell us so much about ourselves.

Fluent in Ancient Greek by the age of 12, she taught herself Sanskrit, and took an interest in Hinduism and Buddhism. As a Christian convert who criticised the Catholic Church and as a communist sympathiser who denounced Stalinism and confronted Trotsky over treacherous party developments,

Weil's independence of mind and resistance to ideological conformity are central to her philosophy.

Several mystical experiences, including Weil's discovery of the poem *'Love (III)'* by the 17th-century poet George Herbert, led her to embrace Christianity. In her book *Devotion* (2017), the Francophile poet and rock star Patti Smith described Weil as 'an admirable model for a multitude of mindsets. Brilliant and privileged, she coursed through the great halls of higher learning, forfeiting all to embark on a difficult path of revolution, revelation, public service, and sacrifice.'

A Weil revival is underway

In recent times, there has been a surge of nationalism, populism and tribalism – Weil had a lot to say about these. She argued that: 'The intelligence is defeated as soon as the expression of one's thought is preceded by the little word *'we'*.'

Uncritical collective thinking holds the free mind captive and does not allow for dissent. She advocated the abolition of all political parties, which, she argued, were totalitarian. To substantiate this claim, Weil offered three arguments:-

1) A political party is a machine to generate collective passions.
2) A political party is an organisation designed to exert collective pressure upon the minds of all its individual members.
3) The first objective and also the ultimate goal of any political party is its own growth, without limit.

These organisations make people stupid, requiring a member to endorse 'a number of positions which he does not know'. Instead, the party thinks on his behalf, which amounts to him 'having no thoughts at all'. People find comfort in the absence of the necessity to think, which is why they so readily join such groups.

What can be done with Weil?

If her psychological complexity makes it difficult to adopt her as a role model, she does provide practical wisdom for teachers, students, workers and citizens.

For outsiders of any gender, creed or colour, she has something to say. She is relentlessly anti-ideological, guiding us against narcissism. She invites us to *act* in the world, and to recognise hypocrisy and denial.

Stressing the urgency to communicate and to *do*, her life can inspire political action. She serves as a muse for anyone open to her mystery. In a society whose most distinct feature is alienation, Simone Weil proposes ways to feel at home again in a place that has become strange.

Additional reading: *The Need for Roots, Gravity and Grace, Intimations of Christianity Among the Ancient Greeks, Notes on Philosophy,* and *On the Abolition of All Political Parties.*

3 Shelagh

Morrissey's idol: Celebrating Shelagh Delaney

Shelagh Delaney was born in 1938 and was raised in Salford, Greater Manchester. She wrote a successful West End play as a teenager.

'*A Taste of Honey*' premiered in 1958, and was an instant success in both London and New York. It was made into a Bafta-winning film in 1961. She wrote it in just two weeks, reworking material that she had previously written for a novel. The play, considered one of the era's best 'kitchen sink' dramas, portrayed working class life in Salford.

The daughter of a bus inspector, Delaney attended Broughton Secondary Modern before transferring to a grammar school. She failed her eleven plus exam four times, but she was ambitious and 'cheeky'.

Speaking to the *New Musical Express* in 1986, the legendary Mancunian singer songwriter Morrissey said: 'I've never made any secret of the fact that at least 50 per cent of my reason for writing can be blamed on Shelagh Delaney.'

TV scriptwriter Tony Warren was also influenced by Delaney's work, and drew on its themes in his best-known creation, *Coronation Street*. The famous soap opera was first screened two years after *A Taste of Honey* hit the stage.

Morrissey used *A Taste Of Honey* as lyrical inspiration with his band *The Smiths* and as a solo artist, including lines in his songs that were lifted directly from Delaney: –

- *And I'll probably never see you again* – (from the song Hand In Glove)
- *I dreamt about you last night / and I fell out of bed twice* and *You're the bees knees / but so am I* – (Reel Around The Fountain)
- *The dream's gone / but the baby's real enough* – (This Night Has Opened My Eyes)
- *Six months is a long time* – (Shoplifters Of The World Unite)
- *It's my life / to ruin / my own way* – (Alma Matters)

Dr Christopher Lee, historian at the *University of Salford*, said the success of Delaney's work is rooted in its controversy.

'At the time scripts were heavily censored. You couldn't swear, or portray homosexuality. *A Taste of Honey* was a story about a pregnant schoolgirl in a relationship with a black sailor. It was real life – that was so special.'

Delaney evaded the censors through 'implying rather than stating, much to the annoyance of middle class playwrights of the time. Here was this schoolgirl living near the docks and beating them at their own game.'

Dr Lee says Delaney's rise was hindered by the conservative attitudes of the time, and because of her gender.

'She tried to open an arts centre, and was side-lined – because she was a woman, and should have been at home having babies.

'But she is up there with the greats. She was one of the most influential playwrights of the century. Her influence is still felt today.'

For fans of *The Smiths*, Delaney needs no introduction. She was a huge influence on the whole of Morrissey's outlook and sensibility, and she graces the cover of the band's 1987 album, *Louder Than Bombs*.

Manchester music historian Paul Wild says Morrissey had huge respect for the kitchen sink dramas of the time. 'Morrissey is from Stretford, and they were a backdrop to his life,' he said.

'He related to all the 'black and whiteness' – it became his style. Even the name *The Smiths* is bland and every-day. He celebrated the bleak.'

Delaney was elected a fellow of the Royal Society of Literature in 1985.

The *National Theatre* revived her play in 2019, and it successfully transferred to *Trafalgar Studios* in 2020.

8th December 2022

4 Hermettes

Hermettes of New York: Come together in glorious isolation

'I shall spend my pension on brandy and summer gloves.'
– *Jenny Joseph, 'Warning'*

After Risa Mickenberg identified herself as a hermette, a female hermit, proudly retreating from the world while living in the heart of New York City, she received lots of emails.

It seemed to defeat the point of the exercise. 'Getting publicity for this is such a ridiculous thing,' she said. It was also tricky to lead a movement of people who want to be by themselves. But she believed in countering a social stigma that made women feel uncomfortable about being alone.

Mickenberg, 55, a playwright and film director, proposed to correct this with a glossy publication, *Hermette Magazine*, 'a lifestyle magazine for aspiring lady hermits' which would do for hermettes what *World of Interiors* does for artful wallpaper, making it 'something that's the dream that people have, instead of being something to be afraid of. Being alone is a wonderful thing.'

Mickenberg first set out her stall as a hermette three years ago, before a gathering of likeminded New Yorkers. 'There is a hermette inside of all of us, waiting to stay in,' she declared. Hermettes would practice DEY, a variation on DIY, which stood for 'Do Everything Yourself,' she said. She suggested the adoption of vows, to never marry or have children. They would think of fashion 'as an avoidance technique. Would a cloak of invisibility be your go-to garment?'

She advised her disciples to 'have big ideas' and work on grand projects and 'keep them to yourself,' unless they wished to share them in the pages of her magazine.

Mickenberg argued that New York was the perfect place for the modern hermette, although the group now has members all over the world, from Scotland, Germany, Mexico, Greece, and India.

Historically, and in the pages of *Le Morte D'Arthur*, hermits, who are usually male, are found deep in the verdant forests, or on the tops of mountains. But mountain tops are terribly crowded these days. 'Have you seen the pictures of Everest?' she said. 'You are never really alone so you have to find a way to be apart from people while being with them.'

New York, in her mind, is the ideal spot for this, offering solitude among a multitude. 'I know someone who said his ideal situation is to be at a party reading a book,' she said. This was what the city offered. 'In New York you can be alone together,' she said.

Susan Hwang, 49, a musician who lives in New York's East Village, said Mickenberg described 'something I have been living. But the way she is framing everything, it's like: 'Oh my god, it sounds cool,' she said. 'Since Risa coined

Hermette, it's creating a glamourous mystique around introversion.'

New York, traditionally, was a place people moved to 'to be anonymous,' she said. 'And there's a special place for weirdos in this city, and a special place for single older women. You see them, women who look frail in their physical bodies, and yet you know they're tough, because you see them climbing the subway stairs through the New York winters, and they've lived on the fifth floor of the same walk-up for 30 years.'

Some might be dressed entirely in lime green, or with 'too much eye shadow in the fashion of their day,' she said. 'I think they're what I've been secretly aspiring to be all this time . . . And I always thought I didn't have any life goals.'

17th June 2022

II – Men

'I saw under the sun, that the race is not to the swift, nor the battle to the strong, neither yet bread to the wise; but time and chance happeneth to them all.'

– Ecclesiastes 9:11

5 Ayer

All Things Visible and Invisible: The lively later life of A.J. Ayer

'The gods do not reveal themselves to everyone.'
– *Homer, Odyssey, 16.161*

Alfred Jules Ayer (1910 to 1989) was one of the most prominent philosophers of the twentieth century.

Known as A.J. Ayer or Freddie, he was quite the establishment celebrity in his time. He married three times and wrote a famous book called *Language, Truth and Logic* (1936) which set out his school of thought, called *Logical Positivism*. Material evidence was all that mattered. His critics refuted this. Oxford Professor Keith Ward once memorably teased, 'Prove that I dreamt of elephants last night.'

Ayer was a committed humanist but was happy enough to say grace before supper at his Oxford college, and to sing along during choral Evensong. He quipped: 'I don't utter falsehoods but I don't mind uttering meaningless statements.'

In 1987, at a party held by the fashion designer Fernando Sanchez, Ayer, then 77, confronted boxer Mike Tyson, who was forcing himself on the then little-known model Naomi Campbell. When Ayer demanded that Tyson stop, saying,

'Unhand that woman', the boxer reportedly asked, 'Do you know who the fuck I am? I'm the heavyweight champion of the world,' to which Ayer replied, 'And I am the former Wykeham Professor of Logic. We are both pre-eminent in our field. I suggest that we talk about this like rational men'. Ayer and Tyson then began to talk, allowing Campbell to slip out.

Near-death experience

The story of Ayer's 'death' became legendary when the renowned atheist choked on a piece of salmon in 1988 in a British hospital. He went into cardiac arrest and technically died for four minutes. After he was resuscitated, Ayer wrote in the *Telegraph* newspaper describing the wondrous images he saw—a beckoning red light and the collapse of space and time. The philosopher suggested that his near-death experience provided 'rather strong evidence that death does not put an end to consciousness.'

He became more pleasant company, according to his wife, Dee: 'Freddie has got so much nicer since he died.'

The story goes that after being diagnosed with pneumonia, he was moved into intensive care in the main wing of London's University College Hospital.

One evening he carelessly tossed some smoked salmon into his throat. It went down the wrong way and the graph recording heartbeats plummeted. The nurse rushed to the rescue, but was unable to prevent his heart from stopping. The doctor later told him that he 'died' for four minutes. In his own words, he describes the vivid experience: –

'I was confronted by a red light, exceedingly bright, and very painful, even when I turned away from it. I was aware that this light was responsible for governing the universe. Among its ministers were two creatures who had been put in charge of space. These ministers periodically inspected space and had recently carried out such an inspection. The laws of nature had ceased to function as they should. I felt that it was up to me to put things right.'

An indication that the experience may have been objectively 'real', was that a mother of a friend of his, who had also gone through a heart attack, remembered that she also 'must stay close to the red light.'

Ayer concludes, 'If our future lives consisted, not in the resurrection of our bodies, but in the continuation of our present experiences, we would then be witnessing the triumph of dualism. My experiences have weakened my conviction that my genuine death, which is due fairly soon, will be the end of me.'

18th August 2022

6 Thomas

500 years of immigration: 1522 – 2022

Sir Thomas More is an Elizabethan play about the life of the Catholic martyr Thomas More, the Lord Chancellor of England during the reign of Henry VIII. The play was written by Anthony Munday and Henry Chettle and revised by several writers. Written in 1591, it depicts events of the 1520s.

The manuscript is especially notable for a three-page handwritten revision attributed to William Shakespeare.

The play dramatises events in More's life, and deals with the rule of law when a mob stirs up anti-immigrant protest. Foreign nationals, who have immigrated to England from Italy, are misbehaving, and treating the citizens of London with abuse and disrespect. This is outraging the workers of London, who decide to join together on Mayday and seek revenge on the newcomers.

London's noblemen ask Sheriff Thomas More, who is popular and respected by the people, to try to calm the civil unrest.

CROWD:
Remove the strangers! Remove the strangers!

(Sir Thomas More, The Lord Chancellor, is sent to appease the crowd.)

MORE:
Grant them removed.
Imagine that you see the wretched strangers,
Their babies at their backs and their poor luggage,
Plodding to the ports and costs for transportation,
And that you sit as kings in your desires,
Authority quite silent by your brawl,
And you in ruff of your opinions clothed;
What had you got? I'll tell you: you had taught
How insolence and strong hand should prevail,
How order should be quelled; and by this pattern
Not one of you should live an aged man,
For other ruffians, as their fancies wrought,
With self-same hand, self reasons, and self-right,
Would shark on you, and men like ravenous fishes
Would feed on one another.

DOLL:
That's as true as the Gospel.

LINCOLN:
This is a sound fellow.

MORE:
What do you to your souls
In doing this? O, desperate as you are,
Wash your foul minds with tears, and those same hands,
That you like rebels lift against the peace,
Lift up for peace, and your unreverent knees,
Make them your feet to kneel to be forgiven!

Tell me but this: what rebel captain,
As mutinies are incident, by his name
Can still the rout? Who will obey a traitor?
Or how can well that proclamation sound,
When there is no addition but a rebel
To qualify a rebel? You'll put down strangers,
Kill them, cut their throats, possess their houses,
And lead the majesty of law in line,
To slip him like a hound.

Say now the king
Should come to banish you.

Whither would you go?
What country, by the nature of your error,
Should give you harbour?

Go you to France or Flanders,
To any German province, to Spain or Portugal,
Nay, anywhere that adheres not to England —
Why, you must needs be strangers: would you be pleased
To find a nation of such barbarous temper,
That, breaking out in hideous violence,
Would not afford you an abode on earth,
Whet their detested knives against your throats.

Spurn you like dogs, and like as if that God
Owed not nor made not you, nor that the claimants
Were not all appropriate to your comforts,
But chartered unto them, what would you think
To be thus used?

This is the strangers case;
And this your mountanish inhumanity.

ALL:

Faith, a says true: let's do as we may be done to.

Sir Ian McKellen performed this Shakespeare monologue regarding immigrants in response to the Trump phenomenon, as well as during his visit to the Oxford Union in 2017, and in his one man show tour, 2019 – 2020.

The handwritten original of this speech is in the *British Library*. In Shakespeare's own hand. His only remaining original manuscript.

19th January 2023

7 Dennis

Vocal balm: The singing cure of the Right Honourable Dennis Skinner

Dennis Skinner is a much loved and respected British former politician who served as the Member of Parliament (MP) for Bolsover, Derbyshire, for 49 years (1970 to 2019).

He is a member of the *Labour Party,* and is known for his left-wing opinions, republican ideals, and sharp humour.

He was famous for heckling in the House of Commons and during the Queen's Speech ceremony, when lawmakers hear the government's agenda announced by the monarch.

Some of his best quips: -

- 2017: 'Get your skates on; first race is half past two', referring to the ceremony clashing with the Queen's annual day out at the Ascot horseraces.
- 2013: After the *Royal Mail* was privatised he caused a stir by shouting '*Royal Mail* for sale. Queen's head privatised.'
- 2000: Skinner shouted: 'Tell her to read the *Guardian*' after the newspaper launched a new campaign calling for Britain to become a republic.

The late Queen Elizabeth was known to have taken these in good humour. Harold Wilson, the Labour Prime Minister (1964 – 1970 and 1974 – 1976) with whom the Queen enjoyed her warmest prime-ministerial relationship, felt privately that her late Majesty was always, deep in her heart, 'a Labour girl'.

Dementia campaigner and singer

Skinner's mother and sister had dementia. Skinner himself, now 91, is razor-sharp, doing the *Killer Sudoku* every day. He began singing old songs to his mother. Remarkably, despite her dementia, she remembered them, and would join in.

Dr Ian Le Guillou, from the *Alzheimer's Society*, says that songs can bring back happy memories and make patients feel empowered and engaged. 'The short-term memory is one of the first things to go, because it's not so ingrained in the brain,' he says.

There's no known cure for dementia, so if a sing-song helps, it has to be worth a try.

So then Skinner started visiting Derbyshire care homes to sing to elderly patients with dementia. This has been known to help them retain some of their rapidly fading memories, often leading group renditions of his mother's favourite, '*Getting to know you.*'

Skinner says he sang in the school choir and would sing in clubs and pubs while working as a coal miner, developing a passion for music.

'If there is a little bit that we can do to enhance their lives. I know that they had a happier time as a result of all of the singing and the use of brain co-ordination with their feet and hands and all the rest of it. I know that those two and a half hours helped those people in that room.'

Dr Le Guillou says that the *Alzheimer's Society* is funding a centre for PhD students to study how arts and music can benefit people with dementia. 'Singing is not only an enjoyable activity, but an excellent way to bring people and their carers together to express themselves and socialise with others. At *Alzheimer's Society*, we often hear of people at our *Singing for the Brain* support groups, not only having fun, but positively relating to music - even when many other memories are hard to recall.'

Susan Drayton, the Clinical Lead for Nursing at *Dementia UK*, agrees that singing is an inclusive activity for patients that can prove calming and enjoyable. Ms Drayton says it also has an effect on recall. 'Music can stimulate the brain and help reconnect someone with a past memory or experience, which can aid communication and improve relationships.'

16th March 2023

8 Nuncle

'Prithee, nuncle, be contented!'
– *Fool (King Lear, III, 4)*

My uncle Christakis passed away in 2019. He was eighty one. He was my mum's brother. He was a pleasure to be around. Funny, sociable, charismatic. He never married. He enjoyed watching football and following politics.

Once, by accident, he sent me a voice message. His phone had somehow dialled my number.

I listened to the recording. The '*message*' is three minutes and seventeen seconds long (3:17). It's an accidental recording of a conversation with some of his neighbours.

It's an endearing exchange about the gardening services provided to their communal garden.

I have kept it on my phone ever since. It's a message from another world. To remind us of him.

It may sound a little mundane, especially to those who didn't know him, but I love its detail, its repetition. The everyday run-of-the-mill-ness of it.

In the first months after his death I used to play it a lot.

May his memory be eternal.

The scene

He is outside his flat in East Finchley. It must have been a nice day.

There are three characters in this play about cutting the grass. It's a good natured exchange, with friendly banter, even though there is disagreement and argument.

The recording went exactly, verbatim, like this.

The dialogue

Christakis: Water it regularly, especially here, this part. We water it. Me and ... what's her name?

Neighbour: Eileen.

Christakis: Eileen. We water it.

Neighbour: The only thing ... I mean, in this weather, it's not good to go too low.

(*The neighbour's accent is hard to place. I'd guess North African / Arabic / Middle Eastern*).

Christakis: That means, it's ... their lawnmower is not good enough.

Neighbour: No. Knife needs to be sharpened more. Because ... they cut it, everything around.

Christakis: *(Tuts.)* Eh... it's the same thing. You say the knife. The lawnmower is not *good* enough. How can you tell me that they cut this grass yesterday?

Neighbour: They did cut.

Christakis: They passed their machine over it, but they didn't cut it.

Neighbour: They did cut because everything around is cut ...

Eileen: What are you shouting about?

Christakis: We are talking, we are not shouting.

Eileen: You're shouting.

(*English. In her eighties. Obviously sitting outside and overhearing this riveting exchange.*)

Christakis: Are you disturbed? (*Chuckles.*)

Eileen: No. (*Also laughing.*)

Neighbour: Everything around was cut ... because ...

Christakis: If you tell me now that this grass was cut yesterday, then you don't know what you are saying, as well. They don't know what they are doing, they don't know what they are saying, and you come to tell me the same thing.

Neighbour: Have a look. Have a look. This grass was cut.

Christakis: I said they passed their lawnmower over it, but they didn't cut the grass properly.

Neighbour: They did cut, but it wasn't cut hundred percent. And the reason was, for example here ...

Christakis: Listen. We talk, and we don't understand each other. You keep to your, ah, theme, and I keep to my theme. (*To Eileen.*) Do you think that this grass was cut yesterday? The grass should be cut like here.

Neighbour: In this weather ...

Christakis: Again, 'in this weather' and 'in this weather.' The weather has nothing to do with it.

Eileen: There's no flowers on here. Things have come up which nobody's seen.

Christakis: This is like a wild field.

Eileen: It is a field. Haven't you ... I mean ... where were you brought up? In a town? Or in the country?

Christakis: In my *village*. And we had beautiful ... and we had beautiful ....

(And here endeth the recording.)

13th April 2023

9 Hitch

'Friends are God's apology for relations.'
– *Christopher Hitchens*

Friday, 13th April, 2012: Martin Amis, Salman Rushdie, Ian McEwan, and James Fenton share their memories of their friend, Christopher Hitchens, with Charlie Rose.

James Fenton: He was a leading figure of the revolutionary left in Oxford. I don't think it's a secret, but he was a very bad Trotskyite. He was on the lazy side. I went to his revolutionary group, which I wasn't yet a member of. They used to meet in rooms above pubs; rooms that were used by an organisation called *The Elks*, with elk horns everywhere. I said the reason Christopher hasn't been coming to the meetings, is that he's been working hard, proselytizing, and here I am as a new member of this group. I saved him from being thrown out of the Trotsky movement.

Ian McEwan: Hitch came to my house two years ago in London. He said, 'Before I come in, before you pour me a drink, there's a woman on the other side of the square being harassed by some yobs. We've got to go across and sort them out.' Martin and I looked at each other. He said, 'There's only seven of them. Come on, there are three of us.' So we set off – two of us very reluctant soldiers in his little private army – and when we got there, thank God there was no-one there, they'd all gone. I think of this story because he was a street fighter. Intellectually, but he also chased villains down the street. He did it in Washington, some mugger he pursued.

Salman Rushdie: I first met Christopher at the Notting Hill Carnival. He was suspicious of me, because I had friends on the Left who were not the kind of Left that Christopher approved of.

James Fenton: What sort of friends do you mean? Name names.

Salman Rushdie: I'm not going to name names! (*Relents.*) ... Tariq Ali. He was relieved to find that I was more suitable than he had feared.

Charlie Rose: Martin, was George Orwell to him what Saul Bellow is for you?

Martin Amis: Maybe. Hitch stressed that Orwell wasn't a genius. His strength was exalted common sense. It's amazing how often Orwell was right, and also to have said the best thing about any number of subjects.

Salman Rushdie: Christopher is a good hater, hating a sequence of people who were worth hating. Henry Kissinger. Mother Teresa. Bill Clinton. They were highly articulated and thought out hatreds.

James Fenton: He liked being rude to people.

Ian McEwan: That's the paradox, a socialist and man of the people, and if you saw how rude he could be to cabbies.

Martin Amis: He'd say to waiters, if you're so smart what are you doing in a dump like this. Or a taxi driver, if you're so smart why are you steering this bed pan around town.

Ian McEwan: We got into a cab together and Hitch said we are going the *Natural History Museum* and the guy was Ukrainian. He said, 'I don't know where it is.' Hitch said, 'We're getting out. You're living in this country you don't know where the *Natural History Museum* is, you don't deserve our fare.' Hitch got out and almost fell over on the pavement, he was so ill. We got another, approved cabbie, who knew where the *Natural History Museum* was.

Charlie Rose: James, write the first line of the obituary.

James Fenton: Oh, to me he was the revolutionary spirit of 1968. He said and did many fine things. So engaging.

10 Women

Camus and his women

Apart from his books, Albert Camus also liked writing love letters: he was an obsessive womaniser whose constant affairs drove his second wife to mental breakdown.

Jean-Paul Sartre was Camus' intellectual sparring partner. When asked which of Camus' books he liked best he said: '*The Fall*, because Camus has hidden himself in it.'

The Algiers slum kid became, at 43, the second youngest Nobel Prize winner in history. Letters published 50 years after his death reveal him as a devoted adulterer.

The Fall (1956) is the confession of a celebrated Parisian lawyer brought to crisis when he fails to come to the aid of a drowning woman. The *'drowning woman'* was Camus' second wife, Francine. Francine said to her husband: 'You owed me that book.' Camus agreed.

In December 1959, Camus' womanising reached its apotheosis.

On December 29th, he wrote to his mistress announcing that he would shortly be returning to Paris from Lourmarin, where he had spent the summer with his wife and children: 'This frightful separation will at least have made us feel more than ever the constant need we have for each other.'

On the next day he wrote: 'Just to let you know I am arriving on Tuesday by car. I am so happy at the idea of seeing you again that I am laughing as I write.'

A day later, he wrote: 'See you Tuesday, my dear, I'm kissing you already and bless you from the bottom of my heart.'

There was yet another letter, setting up a date in New York.

Apart from the candid honesty, there was one thing remarkable about these letters: they were all to different women.

The first was to Mi, a young painter; the second to Catherine Sellers, an actress; the third to Maria Casares, an internationally famous actress with whom he had a liaison for 16 years; and the fourth was to an American, Patricia Blake.

When, over a period of five years, Camus' biographer, Olivier Todd, got access to all of these letters, he faced a dilemma. Copyright of all Camus' letters is invested in his literary executor - his daughter, Catherine. 'It is one thing for children to know their father was a womaniser,' Todd says, 'but quite another to show them proof.'

But Catherine Camus raised no objections.

Mi, who received the first of those December letters, was a young Danish painter. Camus met her in the traditional way, picking her up at the *Café de Flore* in Saint Germain des Pres in 1957. She was one of the rare women with whom he shared his other passion - football.

The Nobel committee gave the Literature prize to a 'Frenchman of Algeria' at a high point in the Algerian war. Camus was instantly derided by most of the Parisian intellectual elite. Decades later, in the sixties, Sartre refused the prize. Unlike Sartre though, Camus condemned Stalin's labour camps when their existence was revealed. He was a diligent journalist working in occupied Paris for the underground paper, *Combat*, while the privileged spokesman for communism, Sartre, led a life of material ease.

Tragically, Camus kept none of these planned rendezvous. Driving back to Paris with his publisher and friend Michel Gallimard, their car hit a tree and he was killed instantly. He was 46.

Far from being a Parisian intellectual with little conscience about his affairs, Camus' relationships were important to him. 'He had a much more healthy relationship with women than Sartre,' Todd says. 'His relationships were quite moving'.

III – Health

'In the depths of winter, I found within myself an invincible summer.'

– Albert Camus

11 Meat

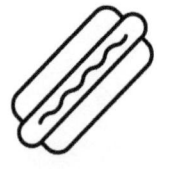

How France has lost its mind

'Fire, woman, and the sea: evils three.'
– *Menander*

The barbecue is an evil that must be stopped for the sake of women, and the environment, according to a new feminist campaign in France.

Sandrine Rousseau, a Green MP, opened the 'barbecue war' by branding the outdoor grill as a ritual that reeks of virility, male meat-eating compulsion and power over women.

'We have to change mentalities so that eating a steak cooked on a barbecue is no longer a symbol of virility,' she told her party, *Europe Ecology*.

Rousseau, an 'eco-feminist' university lecturer with a reputation for controversy, provoked anger from conservatives, President Macron and also from traditional leftists. It came only a week after the Greens, which are part of the main opposition bloc in parliament, suggested banning private swimming pools.

Éric Ciotti, of the Conservative Republicans, called Rousseau 'grotesque', while Nadine Morano, another prominent party member, tweeted: 'That's enough. Stop blaming boys for everything. Stop *deconstructing men.*'

Le Figaro, a conservative newspaper, attacked Rousseau, 50, saying that feminists wanted to ban barbecues 'as the last surviving little ritual of a virility that has been mercilessly pulverised everywhere in our culture.'

Julien Bayou, leader of the Greens, defended the anti-barbecue brigade, calling the outdoor grill an undeniable symbol of virility. Men carried a heavy responsibility for climate change, he said. 'It has been very much proven. Eating meat is more polluting and men eat twice as much red meat and *charcuterie* as women, so, yes there is a gendered approach to behaviour with food,' he said.

The Greens' ally, the radical left *Unbowed France* party, also weighed in against men and barbecues. Clémentine Autain, 49, one of its leaders, denounced the barbecue for its *'virilisme'*. Sociology explained that there was a very big difference between the sexes over meat eating, she said.

In a break with left-wing solidarity, however, the Communists, the traditional working-class party, mocked Rousseau. 'You eat meat according to what you have inside your wallet, not inside your underpants,' Fabien Roussel, the party leader, said. He invited left-wingers to ignore the Greens and join him for the Communists' annual barbecue in Paris.

Dissent also came from Michel Onfray, a celebrity philosopher who veers between hard left and hard right. 'It's ridiculous to say that when you're having a few mates around for a barbecue it's *phallocracy* and a return to the Stone Age,' he said. 'This lady is a university lecturer. It's appalling.'

Libération, the left-wing daily, sympathised with Rousseau. 'It may displease the haters but the meat at the barbecue is well and truly a totem of virility, especially after a summer that has been disastrous from the climate point of view,' it said. It forecast a new division in society 'between meat eaters and those who refuse to wallow in the consumption of cruel and polluting food.'

A defiant Rousseau said men's food emitted 41 per cent more greenhouse gas than women's. Men were overwhelmingly responsible for the evils suffered by society throughout history, from wars and violent crime to climate change, she added.

This ignores and forgets the fact that men hunted to keep their tribe alive and protect the family unit, for tens of thousands of years.

'Whether the victim is a man, a woman or a child, in the overwhelming majority of cases the author of violence remains a man who follows the stereotypes of gender,' she said. 'So it really is virility which produces these deaths and so you really have to question it.'

20th October 2022

12 Now

Ξυν τω δικαίω τον σον ου ταρβώ στρατόν
'With justice on my side, I don't fear anything.'
– *Sophocles*

In 1992, the Dalai Lama, the spiritual leader of Tibet, met with psychologist and neuroscientist Dr Richard Davidson of the University of Wisconsin, and asked him a simple but challenging question.

He wanted to know why brain research and neuroscience was always focused on anxiety, stress, fear and depression. Could the same techniques and tools in modern neurology also be used in enquiries about kindness, compassion, calmness, mindfulness, meditation, tranquility, and focus? He suggested in engaging in neuroscientific research with Tibetan monks – practitioners who have spent years training their mind.

Davidson began his career studying the disturbed mind, and why some people are more vulnerable to life's slings and arrows, and others more resilient. How can we nudge people towards nourishing and nurturing the qualities that promote human flourishing?

He didn't have a good answer for the Dalai Lama's question, but prompted by his challenge, he devised an experiment. In a laboratory, with some volunteers, he placed a metal plate on their wrist, in order to circulate water very rapidly. He then regulated the temperature of the water. At the highest temperature the water is extremely hot and painful.

The participants are placed in an MRI scanner, with neuro-sensors attached to their heads, and are told that they will hear two tones. When they hear the very high pitched tone, they know that in ten seconds they will be zapped with a painful, hot water stimulus. If they hear a low tone, they will just feel mild, warm water instead.

The two groups of people used were those who have meditated regularly, and those who have never meditated, with their age and gender matched.

Meditator v. control groups

Davidson and his team know where in the brain the '*pain circuits*' reside. When looking at those circuits in the 'non-meditating' control group, the moment they hear the high pitched tone, their brain reacts as if they had already received the actual pain. Nothing has happened, at that point, other than they heard a tone.

When they did the same thing with the 'meditator' group, and they received the same high pitched tone, alerting them to the imminent pain … *nothing happened*. There is absolutely no change in the pain matrix – they're flat.

Then when the actual heat comes on, both groups respond, with the pain circuits fully aroused and triggered, as expected. But then as soon as the heat pain goes off, the meditators come right back down to normal baseline. The non-meditators persist – their pain circuits are still reverberating. It's as if they can't shut them off. They're ruminating about the pain.

The non-meditators *perceived* the pain more, even though they had exactly the same amount of *actual* pain as the meditators. This was damaging to the mind's calmness.

The conclusion is that wellbeing is a skill. Wellbeing can be learned. It can be nurtured. The rested mind can then help you focus on the things you can control, and things you can influence, and you can spend time with people who matter to you. The extra strain on the pain circuits also adversely influences your life expectancy.

When human beings first evolved on this planet, none of us brushed our teeth. This is learned behaviour. It's not part of our genome. Davidson adds, 'If we spent the short amount of time that we spend brushing our teeth, nurturing our mind, this world would be a very different place.'

24th November 2022

13 Stoic

Must be, strangely exciting, to watch the stoic squirm

'Well, I knew he was mortal when he was born.'
– *Xenophon, philosopher, 370 BC – on being told that his son had died*

Love, loss, and mortality

Increasing our emotional resilience to loss was the major obsession of the ancient Stoic philosophers, from around 340 BC to the death of Roman emperor Marcus Aurelius in 180 AD. We do this by reducing our attachments, within certain bounds.

The Stoics believed that most of our problems in life are caused by placing too much value on things that are not entirely up to us, and neglecting to pay attention to our own character and actions.

Epictetus (50 – 135 AD), a Stoic philosopher, discusses this in *The Discourses*. He says that the majority of us simply give ourselves more reasons to become upset, 'more causes for lamentation', the more friends we acquire, and the more places with which we fall in love.

'Why then,' he asks, 'do you live to surround yourself with other sorrows upon sorrows through which you are unhappy?'

The word for love that he uses, *philostorgia*, is often translated as '*natural affection*' or '*familial affection*'. It's the kind of love a parent has for their children. In Stoic theology, it's the love that Zeus has for mankind. Stoicism takes that as the exemplar of rational love in general — it's the purest form of love.

Epictetus goes on to tell his students that when they kiss their own brother, friend or child, they should remind themselves that one day the loved one will be gone. (In ancient Greece and Rome it was considered normal for friends to kiss on the lips.) The pleasure of experiencing their presence should be enjoyed along with awareness of their potential absence, and never as though we were taking them for granted.

Memento Mori

Epictetus compares this to 'those who stand behind men in their triumphs and remind them that they are mortal.' He's referring to the ancient tradition whereby generals, or emperors, who had been victorious in battle, would ride through the streets of Rome in a triumphal chariot. Captured enemies and treasure would be paraded before them, to the delight of cheering crowds of onlookers. Their faces would be painted red in emulation of the god Jupiter Optimus Maximus. Slaves would stand behind them holding laurel crowns over their heads, while whispering phrases such as *memento mori*, or 'remember you must die', in their ears.

We should, likewise, remind ourselves that those we love, and kiss, are mortal, and do not, ultimately, belong to us. Like figs or grapes, which are given to humanity by nature when in season, they cannot be ours forever. They are on loan to us from nature.

Continuing this metaphor, anyone who wishes for fresh figs or grapes in winter, is being foolish, by demanding something which would be contrary to nature.

Epictetus tells his students that they should have thoughts like this always ready to hand, night and day. In the same way, they should say that they knew they were mortal themselves, and that they might lose their home, or be thrown into prison.

The greatest peril of misplaced worry, Seneca (4 – 65 AD) cautions, is that in keeping us constantly worrying about an imagined catastrophe, it prevents us from fully living. He amplifies this by compelling us to action: 'The fool, with all his other faults, has this also, he is always getting ready to live.'

9th February 2023

IV – Culture

'Tradition is not the worship of ashes, but the preservation of fire.'

– Gustav Mahler

14 Quiz

Have a go. Pick an answer. How many can you get right?

1. **Which Native American character does Daniel Day-Lewis play in the film '*The Last of the Mohicans*'?**
   Brave Eagle / Hawkeye / Long Rifle / Running Bull
2. **In '*The Matrix*' what colour pill does Neo swallow?**
   White / Blue / Green / Red
3. **Which blockbuster hit movie is loosely based on Henrik Ibsen's play '*An Enemy of the People*'?**
   Jaws / Star Wars / Avatar / Goodfellas
4. **Which TV family's early life is portrayed in the 2021 film '*The Many Saints of Newark*'?**
   The Kardashians / The Simpsons / The Sopranos / The Osbornes
5. **How much did Will Smith earn for his role in '*Men in Black 3*'?**
   $55m / $85m / $100m / $130m
6. **In 1895, 5% of Britain was covered in woodland. What's the percentage % figure today?**
   2.2% / 3.7% / 11.8% / 17.0%
7. **What's the biggest selling song of the 1990s?**
   Wannabe / Baby One More Time / Candle in the Wind / I Will Always Love You

8. **Who's the biggest selling *rap* artist of all time?**
   P Diddy / Eminem / Missy Elliot / Jay Z
9. **In Formula 1, how fast was the fastest ever recorded pit stop?**
   1.82 seconds / 2.62 seconds / 2.97 seconds / 3.66 seconds
10. **Which team holds that record, for the fastest ever F1 pit stop?**
    Mercedes / Red Bull Racing / Ferrari / McLaren Renault
11. **Which was the first ever Olympic Games where *all* countries sent female athletes?**
    Montreal, 1976 / Los Angeles, 1984 / Barcelona, 1992 / London, 2012
12. **Who has *not* won the Nobel Peace Prize?**
    Malala Yousafzai / Nelson Mandela / Mohandas Gandhi / Barack Obama
13. **Who wrote the song lyric: *'I'm bossed up, I got 'em awestruck, It's not a toss-up, I'm the winner'*?**
    Ariana Grande / Lady Gaga / Nicki Minaj / Cardi B
14. **Which book begins: *'It was a bright cold day in April, and the clocks were striking thirteen'***
    Animal Farm / Nineteen Eighty-Four / A Clockwork Orange / Brave New World
15. **Dallow, Spicer, Pinkie and Cubitt are characters in which 1938 novel?**
    The Great Gatsby / Watership Down / Brighton Rock / Brideshead Revisited
16. **What is the population of Bangalore?**
    8 million / 12 million / 16 million / 19 million

17. In a room of 23 people, what is the *percentage chance* that two people share the same birthday?

6% / 18% / 35% / 50%

18. What is Rhinotillexomania?

Chronic nosebleed / Picking your nose / Sneezing uncontrollably from allergies / Over-developed sense of smell

19. What percentage of your bones are in your *feet*?

10% / 17% / 25% / 30%

20. Which letter does *not* appear on the Periodic Table?

J / R / T / Z

21. People born between 1995 and 2010 – Generation Z – have an average attention span of?

18 seconds / 14 seconds / 12 seconds / 8 seconds

22. Which American novel begins: *'It was a queer, sultry summer, the summer they electrocuted the Rosenbergs.'*

The Catcher in the Rye / The Sun Also Rises / The Bell Jar / Catch-22

23. Russia spans how many time zones?

5 / 7 / 9 / 11

24. Who was the first – publicly recorded - politician to kiss a baby during an election campaign?

Pericles, in Athens, 450 BC / John Eaton, U.S. Secretary of War, 1833 / Joseph Goebbels, 1935 / John F. Kennedy, 1960

25. Which organisation has *not* won the Nobel Peace Prize?

Médecins Sans Frontières / The Quakers / European Union / Oxfam

26. Who holds the record – 800 – for the most Test Wickets in cricket.

Wasim Akram / Muttiah Muralitharan / Imran Khan / Shane Warne

27. In a room of 75 people, what's the percentage chance that *two* people share the same birthday?

59% / 69% / 89% / 99%

28. Which democratic assembly was the first to achieve gender parity in its chamber – with equal female and male members?

Iceland / Wales / Denmark / New Zealand

29th September 2022

15 Dragons

Discovering the *Victoria & Albert*

'You might as well go after the dragon.'
– *Dr Jordan B. Peterson*

Fifty years to find the treasure

I have lived in London for around 50 years. My only years away have been my first two in Cyprus, and my three years at the *University of Birmingham*.

It has taken me that long to discover the *Victoria & Albert Museum (V&A)*. I went there for the first time during Easter 2022.

I know exactly why I avoided it for so long. From my youth onwards, I was under the *mistaken* belief that the *V&A* was a twee Victorian museum that housed: wallpaper designs, carpets, dolls, dolls houses, dresses, hats, sewing patterns, porcelain, tea sets, embroidery, haberdashery, wooden furniture, lace, handbags and curtains.

None of this appealed to me. It seemed dusty, uninteresting, feminine.

If any of those kind of things are in there, I didn't see them. Instead I found startling exhibits from all ages. It reminded me of the *Metropolitan Museum* in New York.

Nowadays, going to the *V&A* feels like getting into a warm bath. It has an exact cast replica of Michelangelo's *David*. It was made as a gift for Queen Victoria, from a mould of the original.

It has a Donatello sculpture of St Francis of Assisi. It has magnificent armour and swords. Beautiful, illuminated manuscripts and sacred chant books that are 800 years old.

I tend to go to the *British Museum* and the *Natural History Museum* three or four times a year. The *V&A* will now join them.

Dragons

Probably the most prevalent figure among the museum's 2.3 million artefacts is Christ. My guess is that the second most depicted person is the Virgin Mary. Third, is possibly St George. Happy to be proved wrong.

The *George and the Dragon* story is one of the oldest in folklore. Stephen Fry says that we should teach children this story. Not because dragons exist, but because they can be vanquished.

Prominent psychologist, author and global speaker Jordan Peterson tells the story of his five year old nephew, who had regular nightmares. Peterson says: 'A year after these dreams, his parents were divorced. So there were dragons in the house. The five year old was running around the house all day with a plastic knight's helmet on and a sword, zipping around killing things with it. And at night he'd place the helmet and sword by his pillow. He'd wake up in the night screaming.'

Peterson asked him what he dreamt about. He said he was in a field, and these creatures like dwarves, were coming up to him. They didn't have any arms, they just had legs and big beaks, and they were covered in hair and grease, and there were many of them. And in the distance there was a dragon, puffing out fire and smoke, and the fire and smoke turned into these dwarves.

'What are you going to do about these dwarves? Kill one? Big deal. Ten more are coming', asked Peterson, 'Despite this horror, you could do something about it.'

'Ha,' said the kid. 'I'll take my sword, I'll get my dad, and I'll go to where the dragon was. I'll jump on his head, I'll use my sword to poke both of his eyes out, I'll go down his throat to where the fire comes out, I'll cut a piece of that box out, and I'll use it as a shield.'

'Wow, it's unbelievable', thinks Peterson, that this kid knows that the most sure-fire method of overcoming fears is to confront them.

Psychologists agree that stepping outside your comfort zone is always beneficial.

5th January 2023

V – Music

'**Piano,** *noun.* A parlour utensil for subduing the impenitent visitor. It is operated by pressing the keys of the machine and the spirits of the audience.'

– Ambrose Bierce, The Enlarged Devil's Dictionary

16 Biblical

For every Manc a religion: Biblical language in Manchester's music scene

'I am the resurrection and I am the life.'
– *Stone Roses*

Between 1976 and 1994 the music scene in Manchester grew in prominence, and biblical language was used extensively.

The beginning was very different to the end. Biblical allusions and quotations were used at first in the name of dark introspection, cynical observation, nihilism and pessimism. By the end, such language was about self-congratulation, self-importance, hedonism, and optimism.

Easter 2006 saw the *Manchester Passion*, a public re-enactment of the Gospel story, featuring the music of *The Smiths, Joy Division, New Order, Stone Roses*, and *Happy Mondays*. The distinctive use of biblical sensibility occurs throughout the work of these *big five*.

The Smiths also used religious language and imagery in their effervescent and rumbunctious songs. The *Vicar in a Tutu* may cut a tragic figure, but he just wants to live his life that way. Lead singer Morrissey himself would make a mini-industry from his sacred heart kitsch poses. His solo single *I Have Forgiven Jesus*, highlights personal angst with quintessential irony and humour.

A crucial influence in these trends is Manchester's cityscape. The city had a long cultural history of being portrayed as the archetypical, dour working class city, from the emergence of the hugely popular soap opera *Coronation Street* and black and white films such as *A Taste of Honey*.

The regeneration that Manchester would undergo, from the sky-scraping dominance of the Hilton hotel to countless trendy bars, led to the rave scene of the 1980s and 1990s. These urban changes were led by pioneering figures – like producer and night club owner Anthony H. Wilson – by taking over cheap old buildings for the sake of leisure.

The popular underground Northern Soul movement of the 1960s and 1970s pretty much single-handedly created dance, rave and DJ culture. It spread the Detroit and Motown soul sounds – with their deep roots in *slave spiritual* songs and gospel music – throughout clubs in Wigan, Burnley, Blackpool, Stoke-on-Trent, Blackburn, Preston, Bolton, Rochdale, Runcorn, Warrington, Crewe and Manchester.

Joy Division were influenced by the drum-beats and unconventional sounds in 1970s disco music. They took the guitar riff from Nolan Porter's Northern Soul classic, '*Keep on Keeping on*', for their own '*Interzone*'.

Ian Brown of the *Stone Roses* spoke about his spiritual life, a belief in a higher force, and using 'natural' psychedelic drugs for spiritual insights. He goes to different religious places of worship, and is an avid reader of the Koran and the Bible. He counts the book of *Exodus* as an important influence and is obsessed with the figure of Moses.

The *Stone Roses* quote Christ's injunction that '*the kingdom's all inside*', and the *Happy Mondays* jauntily sing, '*Hallelujah, hallelujah / Not here to praise ya / Just here to raise ya n' fill you full of nails.*'

Religion, particularly Catholicism, forged the identities of Manchester families. Manchester is a city that rose up with the industrial revolution and was built on the cotton trade and immigration, both Jewish and Irish. Catholic immigrants from Ireland contributed to the availability the Bible and its related imagery and language. It's notable that the major players of this scene all had Catholic and Irish Catholic upbringings, from Tony Wilson through to *The Smiths, Happy Mondays,* and *Oasis's* Gallagher brothers.

There was a prominent Jewish population in Prestwich, which Mark E. Smith of independent band *The Fall* had encountered in his youth. Smith formed a multi-faith gang consisting of Protestants, Catholics and Jews as a youngster. The anger and cynicism of 1970s punk music laid the foundation for the more uplifting music of the 1980s and 1990s.

7th July 2022

17 Morrissey

Morrissey and I

'My childhood is streets upon streets upon streets. Streets to define you and streets to confine you.'

– Morrissey, 'Autobiography'

From the start of his career, singer Steven Patrick Morrissey was not like anybody else. He hasn't wavered in 40 years.

At the time of writing, he has created 13 beautiful solo studio albums and 59 singles. His cause has always been the same: the outsider, the neglected, the ignored, the helpless, the marginalised, the awkward, the anxious, the outliers. It just so happens that in 2022, one of those outcast tribes now appears to be white working class men and boys. Today, they're the lowest attaining educational socio-economic group. Someone has to speak for them.

Name one other artist who has recorded a moving song about a disabled girl. Or about a soldier's cry for help. Have a listen to *November Spawned a Monster* and *I Bury the Living* if you don't know them. Spellbinding storytelling and thrilling musical invention.

Escaping his provincial Northern suburbia, he never hid his rejection and distaste for established norms, institutions, royal privilege, political cynicism and the mediocre music industry. His solo music after *The Smiths* has been described by Canadian author Douglas Coupland, as 'punchy rockabilly, glam rock, misfit Americana.'

Mexicana

In early 1991, Morrissey began to cultivate the rockabilly style, a subculture that mirrored the Hispanic greaser lifestyle of Los Angeles – the clothes, the hair.

Chas Smyth of the band *Madness* took Morrissey to the Camden Workers Social Club while he was recording his second solo album *Kill Uncle*. The Camden Workers Social Club exclusively played rockabilly music and the people who attended the club wore 1950s clothes, and splendid quiffs. Morrissey was looking for musicians to take on tour. He met Alain Whyte and Boz Boorer, and hired them. A new look and sound was born.

The archetypal *Smiths* and early Morrissey audiences were teenage school and college kids, 1980s-era goths, and Northern Soulsters. Then in the early nineties there appeared young Mexican men dressed in rolled-up Levi's, Morrissey t-shirts, and biker boots, along with Mexican girls dressed like the Pink Ladies from *Grease*. Of course, the music was central. Panache, longing, drama, aching vocals, and pulsating rhythms.

Professor Melissa Hidalgo, of University College San Diego, wrote a book called, *Mozlandia: Morrissey Fans in the Borderlands*, in 2016. She was drawn to 'both the music and the look. My fandom was about the songs, the music, his brattiness. I loved all that.'

Morrissey these days seems to have a resilient audience of hardcore fans who just love him and don't care what others say. Or even care what *he* says, outside his music.

'Fandom is very personal,' says Hidalgo. 'It's about the self. You're going to like something you like, and no one in the world is going to tell you not to do it. Because if they tell you not to do it, you'll do it even more.'

Litigation

Morrissey sued the *New Musical Express* paper for suggesting he was a racist. They reached a settlement.

The *NME*'s statement read: 'We wish to make it clear that we do not believe we ever called Morrissey a racist and nor do we believe he is. We have said sorry to Morrissey for any misunderstanding that may have arisen.'

Morrissey's lawyer, John Reid, said: 'My client is obviously pleased that the *NME* have publicly apologised to him. This claim was never about financial damages. No money was sought as part of a settlement. The *NME* apology in itself is settlement enough.'

13th October 2022

18 Rollers

Johnny Marr meets Noel Gallagher

Johnny Marr was the lead guitarist in *The Smiths*. He has played with many bands, such as *The Killers* and *Oasis*.

Noel Gallagher was lead guitarist and lead songwriter in *Oasis*.

Johnny Marr: 'I once gave Noel Gallagher a guitar. My brother, Ian, had introduced us. They were just starting out. I'd been to a couple of gigs. And they played to eight people and a dog, sort of thing.

Noel was asking me what I thought of one of the gigs one time.

I said, 'It's great. It's fantastic. But you really need to get another guitar', because he used to stand with his back to the audience, in between songs, tuning up. You could go to the bar and have a drink and he'd still be tuning up. 'Just get one.'

Quite rightly, he said to me, 'Well, that's alright for you to say, I'm on the dole. I've got twelve quid. You've got a hundred guitars. It's all very well, but I'm skint.'

I thought, 'Right, of course, yeah.' So I said, 'I'll lend you one of mine.' And his eyes lit up.

I had this sunburst-coloured 1960 *Les Paul*. Worth a fortune. It got it from Pete Townsend.

No-one knew them as this time.

That became his main guitar.

They took off very quickly after that. They got a lot of attention. A few weeks passed, and I read in the music press, '*Johnny Marr Gives Band Guitar.*'

The way he'd made it out was that he and I met on this grassy knoll at midnight, under a full moon. In our shades. And that I'd walked up onto the knoll and passed him the *Les Paul,* like *Excalibur*. And said, 'Here. Keeper of the flame. Taketh thy *Les Paul* and lay down some heavy licks. That the masses may fall at your feet. And you will become King Noel. Arise, King Noel.' And then we drank the blood of a groupie.

Which isn't actually what happened. I said, 'You can borrow this guitar for a bit. Until you get some money.'

Anyway, he fell in love with this guitar, and I didn't really have the heart to ask for it back, then.

I know he wrote *Live Forever* on it. It's on the *Live Forever* video.

A few months later, they were starting to get quite big then, they did a gig at Newcastle's *Mayfair*, before it closed down. I get this phone call from the office one morning, totally freaking out, saying, 'Noel has broken the guitar.'

Someone had got up on stage, and started fighting with Liam. And Noel whacked them over the head with this guitar, and broke the guitar.

I was like, 'That's terrible. What do you want me to do about it?'

'Can you lend him another one?'

Right. So. I went and looked through my guitars, and I got this black *Les Paul* that I wrote *Bigmouth Strikes Again* on, and *The Queen Is Dead*.

Noel was freaking out because he thought I'd be really mad, but also because they needed a guitar for the next night.

So I sent this guitar up with a note, saying, 'This one's well heavy. And if you can get a good swing with this one, next time, you'll take the fucker out.'

Years later, 2003 or 2004 I think it was, I was playing on an *Oasis* album. I was at the mixing desk listening to the track. And Jason, who used to be my roadie, and was now Noel's roadie, handed me a guitar. I was distracted listening to the track. Jason goes, 'Here.' I put my hand out and it was that black guitar, the second one that I gave him.

So I plugged it in, and played this solo. So it had a nice little resolve to it.

Noel Gallagher meets Keith Richards

Noel was at a hotel for New Year's Eve. Keith Richards was in the same hotel. Keith's kids were massive *Oasis* fans, and already knew Noel. They said, 'Come and meet dad.'

So he did.

'I went to the bar, and there's Keith, looking like a pirate – with three belts, and a sword, and a parrot on his shoulder.

And he looks over, and he says to me, 'Oh, you're still around, are ya?

I said, yeah. And then he says, 'Ere, there's something I've always been meaning to ask ya.'

'Go on'

'Who's the bigger cunt, your singer or mine?'

'And I said, well, since your singer wrote some of the greatest lyrics of all time, I'm gonna have to say mine.'

'I thought as much,' grows Richards.

VI – Drama

'What a world! What a world!'

– Wicked Witch of the West

19 Assassin

The day the music died

The Father and the Assassin*, at the *National Theatre

'India's a rascal that's been around 10,000 years. The British had no idea what they were dealing with.'
– *Overheard at the National Theatre, 30th May 2022*

Nathuram Godse was hanged on 15th November 1949, at Ambala Central Jail, in East Punjab, India. He was tried and found guilty of the assassination of Mohandas Gandhi on 30th January 1948.

His life is brought vividly to the stage with an astounding play by Anupama Chandrasekhar. *The Father and the Assassin* is a damned good evening. Chandrasekhar is one of India's most exciting playwrights, and takes this compelling backdrop of the birth of a nation, to explain Godse's upbringing, political awakening and tragic destiny.

Godse's parents had three sons before he was born, all of whom died early in childhood. Believing that boys were cursed in their family, they brought up Godse for a few years as a girl. His identity was confused until he found politics and nationalism.

Godse had plotted the assassination with Narayan Apte and six others. After a trial that lasted over a year, Godse was sentenced to death on 8th November 1949. Although pleas for clemency were made by Gandhi's two sons, Manilal and Ramdas Gandhi, they were turned down by India's Prime Minister Jawaharlal Nehru, and by the Deputy Prime Minister Vallabhbhai Patel.

The great soul

Gandhi was known as the father of the nation. He was pragmatic, head-strong but also understood symbolism and the psyche and soul of the Indian village. After air and water, salt is a basic human need. Homer said its properties were divine. Gandhi's famous salt march started out with just 80 followers, but then turned into a 60,000 strong juggernaut. It was peaceful resistance like this that drove out the British, in favour of *swaraj* — home rule.

To others, Gandhi was a traitor. 'Every birth requires blood, Mr Gandhi', so said Muhammad Ali Jinnah, the father of Pakistan. Gandhi was unable to convince Nehru, Patel and Jinnah that Muslims and Hindus had co-existed for thousands of years, and should continue to do so, and reluctantly allowed for the creation of Pakistan. It was giving Indian land to this new Muslim nation, at the moment India itself was born, that angered Hindu nationalists like Godse.

It's a colourful, energetic play. An epic story of Greek tragedy proportions — crowds acting as the Chorus, punctuate the tale. The *hubris* of an urgent uprising. And the *nemesis* of political division and ideological schisms. Paul Bazley is charismatic as Gandhi. Laughing, joking, filling the stage. He's brilliant.

It's intensely theatrical. The vibrant colours of India are displayed — the costumes are tamarind, paprika, cinnamon, sunset yellow. The whole cast is superb.

Attempts at image rehabilitation

Godse was a member of the *Hindu Mahasabha* political party, and for a while he was an ardent follower of Gandhi. He then began ridiculing the philosophy of non-violence. He believed Gandhi to have favoured the political demands of the minority Muslims during the partition of India.

In 2014, the *Hindu Mahasabha* party began attempts to rehabilitate Godse and portray him as a patriot. It requested Prime Minister Narendra Modi to install the bust of Godse. In May 2019, in the lead up to the final phase of Indian elections, a candidate from Bhopal, Pragya Thakur, called Godse a 'patriot'. Facing intense backlash, she apologised later.

As Hindu nationalism becomes more widespread in India, statues and temples are being raised in Godse's honour. The city of Meerut was proposed to be renamed after him but the possibility of such a name change was ruled out by the District Magistrate.

Godse and Gandhi share the stage at the end of the play.

Gandhi: One day, people will lose their fear, then all the bullets in the world won't matter. What will you do with your hatred then?

Godse: It's better to be a Godse than a Gandhi ... A Gandhi is of no use to you when tomorrow's battles are fought with deadlier weapons. No, you'll need a Godse. And I will rise.

30th June 2022

20 List

The only movie list you'll ever need.

8½, 21 Grams, The 39 Steps.

All of Me, All the President's Men, Alphaville, Amadeus, Amelie, American Beauty, American History X, American Psycho, Amores Perros, Annie Hall, The Apartment, Apocalypse Now, Arsenic and Old Lace, Argo, Au Revoir Les Enfants.

Bananas, Bande à part, Barefoot in the Park, Barry Lyndon, Barton Fink, Battleship Potemkin, Bicycle Thieves, The Big Heat, The Big Lebowski, The Big Short, The Birdcage, Birdman, The Breakfast Club, Breathless, Brighton Beach Memoirs, Brooklyn, Bugsy Malone, Butch Cassidy and the Sundance Kid.

Carnage, Casablanca, Catch-22, Citizen Kane, A Clockwork Orange, Cold Mountain, Collateral, Control Room, The Corporation, Crash, Crimes and Misdemeanours.

A Day at the Races, Dawn of the Planet of the Apes, The Death of Stalin, The Deer Hunter, Denial, Delicatessen, The Departed, Dial M for Murder, Do the Right Thing, Dog Day Afternoon, Double Indemnity, The Double Life of Veronique, Dr Strangelove, The Dresser, Duck Soup.

East is East, Educating Rita, The Elephant Man, The English Patient, Erin Brockovich, The Exorcist.

Falling Down, Fargo, Ferris Bueller's Day Off, A Few Good Men, Fiddler on the Roof, Fight Club, The Fog of War, Frances Ha, Francis: God's Jester.

Gandhi, Glengarry Glen Ross, The Godfather, The Godfather, Part II, Goodfellas, Good Vibrations, Good Will Hunting, The Gospel According to St. Matthew, The Graduate, Gravity, The Great Dictator, Grosse Point Blank, Groundhog Day, Guess Who's Coming to Dinner.

Hannah and Her Sisters, Hearts of Darkness, His Girl Friday, Horse Feathers, The Hours, The Hudsucker Proxy, The Hurt Locker, Husbands and Wives.

The Idiots, In Bruges, Inception, The Insider, Insomnia, Inglourious Basterds, Intolerable Cruelty, Irma La Douce, Isle of Dogs, It's a Wonderful Life.

Jaws, Jesus of Montreal, JFK, The Journey, Jules et Jim.

Kandahar, The King's Speech, Koyanisqaatsi.

Le Mépris, La Dolce Vita, La Grande Illusion, La Regle du Jeu, La Strada, Lantana, The Last of the Mohicans, The Last Temptation of Christ, Lawrence of Arabia, Le Samourai, Lessons of Darkness, Letters from Iwo Jima, Life is Beautiful, Lost in Translation, Love and Death.

M, The Maltese Falcon, Man Bites Dog, Manhattan, The Man Who Would Be King, Marathon Man, Margin Call, The Matrix, A Matter of Life and Death, Max, Mean Streets, Midnight Run, Mighty Aphrodite, Million Dollar Baby, Mishima, Moulin Rouge, Mr Death, My Best Friend's Wedding, My Fair Lady.

Napoleon Dynamite, Network, A Night at the Opera, Night of the Iguana, Ninotchka, Nixon, No End in Sight, North By Northwest.

O Brother Where Art Thou, Ocean's 11, The Odd Couple, On the Waterfront, Once Upon a Time in Hollywood, One-Two-Three.

Panic Room, Parasite, The Passion of Joan of Arc, The Passion of the Christ, The Phone Call, Pi, Platoon, Play It Again, Sam, The Producers, Psycho, Pulp Fiction, Punch-Drunk Love, The Purple Rose of Cairo.

Raging Bull, Raising Arizona, Ran, Rashomon, Rear Window, Red Dragon, Reservoir Dogs, Richard III, The Right Stuff, Rise of the Planet of the Apes, The Road to Perdition, Robocop, Romeo and Juliet, Romy and Michele's High School Reunion, A Room with a View.

The Sacrifice, Scarface, Seven Samurai, The Seventh Seal, Sexy Beast, Shakespeare in Love, The Shawshank Redemption, The Shipping News, Shoah, Sicario, Sicario 2, Sicko, Sideways, Silver Linings Playbook, Sleeper, The Social Network, Some Like It Hot, South Park – The Movie, Stalag 17, Steve Jobs, Strangers on a Train, Subway, Sunset Boulevard, Sweet Home Alabama, Swimming To Cambodia.

The Taking of Pelham 1-2-3, Taxi Driver, Team America: World Police, The Thin Blue Line, This Is Spinal Tap, Throne of Blood, Tokyo Story, Twelve Angry Men, Two Strangers Who Meet Five Times.

Unbreakable, Uncut Gems.

Vertigo, Vice.

War for the Planet of the Apes, When Harry Met Sally, Withnail & I, Witness for the Prosecution, The Wizard of Oz, The Wrestler.

Yojimbo.

Zero Dark Thirty, Zootropolis, Zorba the Greek.

21st July 2022

21 Patriots

***Patriots*: A play by Peter Morgan**
Almeida Theatre, 2 July to 18 August 2022

'Russia is a riddle, wrapped in a mystery, inside an enigma.'
– Winston Churchill, 1939

New empire

A brilliant evening among Islington's theatre-going literati: all red chinos and tasselled loafers.

This is the story of Boris Berezovsky. Russian oligarch, kingmaker, mentor, and eventually enemy number one of Vladimir Vladimirovich Putin.

It's an epic battle: politicians versus businessmen, the state versus capital.

Putin begins to despise these powerful oligarchs and their decadence. He thinks they're only out for themselves. Berezovsky thinks the opposite: these billionaires are Russia's only chance of avoiding the slide back into the communist dark ages.

They're both right. Russia resembles the England of old – kings so remote from their subjects that 'Robber Barons' were needed to oversee commerce, employ the populace, finance wars and keep society afloat. England evolved out of that in the 15th Century. Russia still operates on that model.

The most heart stopping feeling for me was this: I found Putin pretty sympathetic. Incorruptible, dutiful and steadfast as the mild Deputy Mayor of St Petersburg. The problem is when he crosses the line between patriotism and nationalism.

Characters

Peter Morgan (playwright, screenwriter): I wrote this play. I also wrote *The Crown, Frost/Nixon, The Queen, The Damned United* and *Longford.* I write like an angel.

Boris Berezovsky: I was a Maths prodigy and wrote academic papers on decision theory and risk. It gave me insights into rational and irrational agents.

When Russia begins to liberalise after Gorbachev, I go into business and become super rich. I buy the Russian television channel *ORT,* and it becomes the mouthpiece of Presidents Boris Yeltsin and then Putin. I get a seat in the parliamentary Duma. President Yeltsin asks my opinion on everything, including who should succeed him.

I have my weaknesses. Two ex-wives. And young girlfriends. In the play, one of them calls me from St Moritz telling me it's her birthday. She gives me two numbers. First, her age – which is a third of mine. Second, the amount she's spending on a diamond necklace.

I fall out with Putin and I'm exiled to London.

I'm played by Tom Hollander, energetically. He was in Armando Iannucci's film *In the Loop* as Secretary of State for International Development.

Vladimir Putin: I'm played chillingly well by Will Keen. As a lowly provincial official I allow Berezovsky to open a Mercedes dealership in St Petersburg and in return he introduces me to President Yeltsin. He pulls my strings for many years.

Roman Abramovich: I'm the new kid on the block and become Berezovsky's protege. We grow the newly 'privatised' oil company *Sibneft*. As Putin ascends the ranks, I'm appointed governor of *Chukotka*, Russia's easternmost province. I do well, building schools and hospitals.

Alexander Litvinenko: I'm the most sympathetic and decent character of the evening. I initially refuse Berezovsky's offer to become his head of security for triple my secret service salary. When my superiors give me orders to assassinate Berezovsky, I go public with this, and I join him in London. Eventually, the Russian state catches up with me – killing me with radioactive polonium.

In the play, when I say: 'I'm off to meet someone for tea', there's a gasp of recognition from the audience. I'm played movingly by Jamaal Westman, in an honest, working man, Scouse accent.

True story: I saw Boris Berezovsky once. I was walking down New Bond Street, and saw him looking into the window display of a high end jeweller — *Asprey* or *Bulgari* or somesuch. He was surrounded by four enormous private security guards. He was, no doubt, picking out an item for a mistress.

4th August 2022

22 Elvis

Of all the famous images preserved in the *US Library of Congress National Archives*, the most requested photograph of all time… is Elvis Presley with President Richard Nixon. 'You dress funny', said Nixon.

Nixon eventually warmed to the most famous man on the planet. 'You and me, we rose from nothing. But look where I am today and look where you are today.'

Baz Luhrmann makes very energetic films – *Romeo and Juliet, Moulin Rouge, The Great Gatsby*. John Landis — the director of *Trading Places, The Blues Brothers* and *Coming to America* — found *Moulin Rouge* so breathless and fast, that he said the director should trust his leading actors more, and allow them more screen time. His memorable criticism of the relentless jump cuts was: 'just put the fucking scissors down'.

You get this exact same feeling in Luhrmann's *Elvis*. The scenes have that frenetic pace and intensity — from the rural Gospel music tent gatherings, where Elvis learns his signature hip and knee movement, to the heady heights of his Las Vegas residency — the camera doesn't stand still. This time the manic energy matches its subject. The 'spirit possession' of the Gospel music congregation, transfers to the young women in his first audiences, who scream in an involuntary reflex reaction. The underwear thrown onto the stage soon followed.

It's a brilliant film. A colourful and sensory experience.

Presley repeatedly says that the music that he always went back to, and 'makes me happy' is Gospel and Blues. He recorded an album of Gospel songs called *'How Great Thou Art'* in 1967. The album earned Presley a *Grammy* Award for Best Sacred Performance and a Billboard top 20 pop hit.

Austin Butler's central performance is so convincing in manner, look and voice that you never doubt it's Elvis. Some vintage looking footage looks so real you have to double take to check it's Butler rather than the man himself. The early Elvis is credible enough, but late Elvis is remarkably realistic.

In the last scene, the real Elvis – unwell, loaded with drugs, slurring his words – sits down to sing *Unchained Melody*. The voice and energy are palpable. His mother always brushed aside criticism that he was corrupting the youth with his bodily movements and singing style. She said it was a God-given talent, so there can't be anything wrong with it. With that last blast, in June 1977, just two months before he died, you see what she meant. An operatic, epic performance.

All music biographies have classic ingredients. The manager / fraudster, the friends / hangers on, and the groupies. The easy access to hedonism's heights and valleys – drugs, drink and carnage. Colonel Tom Parker as the promoter, played by Tom Hanks, looms like a ghostly spirit who spots the talent, nurtures it and invents merchandising. Championing a talent, and exploiting it – it's a fine line.

We all have our vices. At the time of Presley's death, Parker owed the *Las Vegas Hilton Hotel* over $30 million in gambling debts. After a lifetime that saw him earn in excess of $100 million, Parker's estate was barely worth $1 million when he died.

There's the inevitable decline — paranoia, delusion, isolation and health degeneration. It's handled with sensitive speed. Kevin Macdonald's documentary film *Whitney* (2018) was dark and matter of fact in its depiction of Whitney Houston's final decline. Surrounded by sycophants, friends and family, all of whom were on the payroll, but none of whom could stop the train crash – chiefly because there was so much gravy on it for them to consume. That same formula is the Elvis story.

8th September 2022

23 Antigone

A preview of Sophocles' 'Antigone': The Burial at Thebes

'When a river bursts its banks, the trees that bend, survive, the trees that stand firm, snap.'
– *Haemon, in 'Antigone'*

I had booked to see this play in April 2020, but the theatre announced that the performances would be cancelled, due to the Covid lockdown.

The place is Thebes (*Thiva* in Greek). A day's walk and 60 km north of Athens. Antigone meets her sister Ismene, in the dead of night, saying she wants to bury her dead brother. He is Polyneices, and he has fallen, fatally, following a fight, with his brother Eteocles.

The King of Thebes, her uncle Creon, decrees that Polyneices is a traitor, and legislates that he should be left unburied, to be devoured by the dogs, and the crows. Whereas Eteocles, by contrast, should be buried with full honours.

In rebellion against this edict, Antigone's deep-rooted tradition, fraternal loyalty, moral code, sacred duty, religious observance, inherited ritual, familial legacy, profound freedom, ethical compass and her connection to a community fabric, all tell her that burying him is the right thing to do.

Antigone, Ismene and their brothers are children of Oedipus and Jocasta, cursed from the tragic fate of incest. Antigone and Ismene supported their blind father on his last journey to Athens where he died peacefully (events played out beautifully in Sophocles' play *Oedipus at Colonus*). They returned home to Thebes, where this play pits them against Jocasta's brother King Creon.

Thus Sophocles sets up the eternal battle between duty and law, between ethics and order, between humility and pride. In this third play of his *Theban trilogy*, the greatest Athenian playwright bestows upon us the divine heroine Antigone who acts as the conscience of the audience, in a colossal, brutal, verbal and moral battle with the tyrant Creon. Meditating between them is her betrothed, Haemon, who is Creon's son. This is the blueprint relationship for Shakespeare's starcrossed lovers Romeo and Juliet. Haemon and Antigone experience the fearful passage of their own death-marked love, with Thebes being the template for Shakespeare's Verona.

This production is based on the poet and Nobel laureate Seamus Heaney's translation of Sophocles' *Antigone,* that tells the epic tale that has inspired politicians, activists and writers for two and a half millennia.

Antigone breaks the law and buries her brother. Her unclean civil hands honour the gods, her conscience, and her bloodline. She is caught and arrested for this carnal, sensual act. What follows is one of the most muscular, dramatic and intense verbal tussles ever written. It's a supreme masterpiece of dramatic theatre, that has haunted audiences ever since. 'I was born to love, not hate', says Antigone, resolute and courageous in her new mutiny.

Antigone is a heroine for all times, a rock of ages. Her soul is greater than the ocean, and her spirit is stronger than the sea's embrace.

Sophocles lived between 496 to 405 BC and wrote over 100 plays. Only seven of them survive today. They are *Oedipus the King, Oedipus at Colonus, Antigone, Ajax, Philoctetes, Women of Trachis* and *Electra*.

He is regarded as one of the three great dramatists of Ancient Greece, along with Euripides and Aeschylus. An overused phrase these days is: 'being on the right side of history'. It's a transient judgment. But when it comes to the Ancient Greeks, and to Antigone, you begin to realise what it really means.

11th April 2020

24 Jeanne

***The Passion of Joan of Arc (1928).* Directed by Carl Theodor Dreyer**
***British Film Institute*, 15th March 2023**

'Jeane, I'm not sure what happiness means,
But I look in your eyes,
And I know.'
– *The Smiths, Jeane*

Teenage kicks

In 1431, a nineteen year old French military leader was tried and convicted for heresy in Rouen, Normandy. The court proceedings were held in the King of England's military headquarters and capital in France – a trial that has arguably become the third most important in history – after the trials of Christ and Socrates.

The young woman who was examined, tried and condemned has been the central character in a whole literature of controversy. Shakespeare, Voltaire, Mark Twain, George Bernard Shaw, and Thomas Paine have demonstrated her as a dynamic and challenging figure.

The English were stricken with fear at her success, and when she was captured, they condemned her as a witch and apostate. Bernard Shaw hailed her as the first Nationalist and the first Protestant.

Jeanne d'Arc was burned at the stake on May 30, 1431. The verdict was later nullified at her rehabilitation trial in 1456. Considered a French national heroine, she was declared a saint by the Roman Catholic Church in 1920.

Cinematic canon

The Passion of Joan of Arc (*French: La Passion de Jeanne d'Arc*) is a 1928 French silent film, based on the actual, verbatim record of her trial. The film was directed by Carl Theodor Dreyer, and starts Renée Maria Falconetti as Joan. It is widely regarded as a major landmark of cinema.

For Falconetti, the performance was an ordeal. Legends from the set tell of Dreyer forcing her to kneel painfully on stone and then wipe all expression from her face — so that the viewer would read suppressed or inner pain. He filmed the same shots repeatedly, hoping that in the editing room he could find the precise nuance in her facial expression.

Reception

The film was an instant critical success and immediately called a masterpiece. It was banned in Britain for its portrayal of crude English soldiers who mock and torment Joan in scenes that mirror biblical accounts of Christ's mocking at the hands of the Roman soldiers.

The film and Falconetti's performance have continued to be praised by critics. The legendary film critic of *The New Yorker,* Pauline Kael, wrote that Falconetti's portrayal 'may be the finest performance ever recorded on film.' Critic Roger Ebert said that 'you cannot know the history of film unless you know the face of Renée Maria Falconetti.'

Numerous respected publications (*The Village Voice, Cahiers du cinema*, and *Sight & Sound*) have consistently listed the film among the greatest of all time – it's normally in the top 10. Michael Mann called it a 'human experience conveyed purely from the visualisation of the human face: no one else has composed and realised human beings quite like Dreyer in *The Passion of Joan of Arc.*'

It is arguably the most influential film of all time, alongside Sergei Eisenstein's *Battleship Potemkin* (1925). Falconetti's performance was ranked 26th in *Premiere* magazine's 100 Greatest Performances of All Time, the highest of any silent performance on the list.

Scenes from the film appear in Jean-Luc Godard's *Vivre sa Vie* (1962), in which the protagonist Nana sees the film at a cinema and weeps as she identifies with Joan. In *Henry & June*, Henry Miller is shown watching the last scenes of the film and in voice-over narrates a letter to Anaïs Nin comparing her to Joan and himself to the 'mad monk' character played by playwright Antonin Artaud.

It's a thing of beauty.

17th May, 2023

VII – Technology

'Computers are useless. They can only give you answers.'
— *Pablo Picasso*

25 Quakes

Drilling for oil and gas: And causing earthquakes

Dutch residents lose patience after years of tremors

The northern tip of the Netherlands has for decades been blighted by earthquakes. They have been triggered by gas extraction from the Groningen gas field.

The field was discovered in 1959 and is the largest in Europe. The frequency and magnitude of the earthquakes has been increasing, damaging houses and infrastructure and agitating local communities. They blame the government and two of the world's biggest energy companies for billions of Euros worth of damage.

The tremors are a reminder of the toll that energy production can have on those living in resource-rich areas. The US state of Oklahoma has experienced earthquakes connected with its shale boom. But it is sparsely populated.

In Groningen, as gas is tapped from ageing reservoirs, pressure falls in the porous sandstone deep underground, leading to compression in the rock. If this occurs along natural fault-lines, it can lead to tension and shocks.

Although the earthquakes are small by international standards, the flatness of the Groningen area means that buildings are unable to withstand even light tremors. Almost 1,380 seismic events have occurred in the Netherlands since 1991, according to the country's statistics agency. The link with gas exploitation cannot always be proven.

For years field operator *Nederlandse Aardolie Maatschappij (NAM),* a joint venture of Shell and ExxonMobil, failed to recognise the earthquake risks associated with production. The state, the gas field's ultimate owner, came under fire for siding with *NAM.*

A turning point was a 3.6-magnitude earthquake in 2012, that damaged thousands of houses. Dutch authorities then moved to limit the tremors by reducing output.

A 2015 *Dutch Safety Board* report concluded the field's operators had 'failed to act with due care for citizen safety' and questioned risk-assessment measures. The government and *NAM* acknowledged the findings.

'*NAM* should have been more eager to learn more about the Groningen subsurface and the earthquakes' impact above the surface,' the operator told the *Financial Times*. '*NAM* regrets that it did not launch a systematic effort to understand safety risks related to earthquakes any earlier.'

The same year, following a lawsuit, a court ruled that *NAM* must compensate homeowners for any drop in house prices caused by earthquakes.

Further tremors and seismic events since have triggered fresh calls for a complete production halt.

Henk Nijboer, a politician with the opposition Labour party, estimates that 90,000 houses need to be rebuilt in the Groningen area and that damage could exceed €10bn. 'The politicians ignored the problem because they shared the same interests as the companies,' he says.

The government is in a difficult spot as it seeks to balance energy security with public safety and financial concerns. More than 80 per cent of extraction profits of the field go to the state and income from gas production — the majority from Groningen — accounts for a tenth of state earnings. Export deals are in place with Germany, Belgium and France. Most Dutch homes use Groningen gas.

For the local community, relations with the government and operators are not helped by the complex process of claiming compensation, involving corporate lawyers. There are disputes about what qualifies as a legitimate claim.

Maarten Wetselaar, Shell's director of integrated gas and new energies, acknowledged that tens of thousands of damages claims had to be paid more quickly and arrangements needed to be made to rebuild and strengthen houses. '*NAM* never intended for its gas production to be harmful to anybody', he said. An ExxonMobil spokesperson said: 'It is crystal clear to us that tremor-related damage has to be compensated.'

9th June 2022

26 Africa

The mobile banking transformation

It has taken us 20 plus years in the UK to move from banking in high street branches, to telephone banking, to Internet banks, and now to mobile phone transactions.

Africa has accelerated this leap, and gone straight to flip-phone banking in a few short years.

Imagine you live in a rural village in Kenya. Your daughter attends university in Nairobi and needs financial support to buy textbooks and pay her rent. How do you send her money if you don't have a bank account or internet access?

In the UK or the US, the answer would be PayPal, Venmo, or online banking. Two billion 'unbanked' adults in developing countries face barriers to simply receiving wages or sending money to family. Their finances are unstable because they don't have a good way to save for the future or borrow in times of need.

Getting people access to formal financial services is called *financial inclusion* and it is a critical part of equitable economic development, says Jay Rosengard, Lecturer in Public Policy at the *Harvard Kennedy School*.

Financial inclusion can be particularly powerful for women and other marginalised groups who have been excluded from the formal economy and have less control over their finances.

When up to 90% of your population doesn't have a bank account, how do you bring them into the financial system?

With mobile banking, the share of Kenyans with access to a financial account jumped from 42% in 2011 to 75% in 2014. Financial inclusion skyrocketed among the poorest citizens, from 21% of people with a financial account in 2011 to 63% in 2014.

'The magic of mobile banking lies in its simplicity and low cost,' said Rosengard. 'All you need to get started is an old flip phone, for less than $10 U.S. dollars, and a SIM card. You can send and receive money over text message, no smartphone or special app are required.'

On *Safaricom's M-PESA*, 19 million users now send 15 billion Kenyan shillings in payments each day – the equivalent of $150 million U.S. dollars. The share of people with access to a financial account in Kenya is double that of other sub-Saharan African countries and triple the rate in low-income countries worldwide.

This has created financial stability for Kenyan families. People were able to handle major hits to their income – a bad harvest, a job loss, or a failing business – without having to reduce household consumption. The primary way was by getting help from family and friends through funds sent over *M-PESA*. In comparison, Kenyans who did not use *M-PESA* had to reduce their household spending by an average of 7% in response to financial challenges.

For developing countries with limited banking, Rosengard sees mobile banking as a shortcut to financial inclusion.

Rosengard explained how, instead of growing the conventional banking sector's physical presence and slowly bringing the 'unbanked' into the system, mobile banking allows countries to immediately bring financial services to the masses in a cheap way.

Cell phones also had this impact in sub-Saharan Africa in the 2000s. Countries were able to skip over the landline telephone phase and rapidly bring modern communication to their citizens. The rate of cell phone ownership in Kenya (82%) is almost as high as in the United States (89%).

'Mobile banking could mean the difference between students dropping out to work or graduating, securing a better career, and being able to send money back home,' Rosengard said. 'Now multiply that impact by the two billion other unbanked people globally, offering a path to inclusive economic growth.'

15th December 2022

27 Magic

Artificial Intelligence: the beginning of the end, or the end of the beginning?

'Any sufficiently advanced technology is indistinguishable from magic.'
– *Arthur C. Clarke*

Artificial Intelligence (A.I.) is upon us.

The AI application *ChatGPT* recently set a record for the fastest app to reach 100 million users. It achieved this in just 2 months. This surpassed *Google+*, which took one year and two months to reach that milestone.

Since its launch in November 2022, *ChatGPT* has taken the world by storm. It is now used by 120m people. A sizeable proportion of that is students.

GPT stands for *Generative Pre-trained Transformer*. Its stellar success has placed an eye-watering valuation of $29 billion on its author company *OpenAI*.

It's simple. You type in a question, and it answers it. It will write out a clear, structured and correct answer in seconds. It will think and rank its answers before it starts typing.

These systems are variously described as algorithms, or Machine Learning (ML), or Natural Language Processing (NLP), or Conversational AI. They are developing at such a fast rate that we struggle to distinguish the real from the imagined. The implications for learning, education and teaching are immense. But we are still in the stone age.

A real demonstration

Here are a few questions that I typed into *ChatGPT*.

1. Write a weather report in the style of a Dr Martin Luther King speech.
2. Does Hamlet suffer from a mental disorder?
3. What lessons can we draw from the fall of the Soviet Union?
4. Write a song about school exams in the style of Stormzy.
5. If a plus b is 8, and the difference between a and b is 3, what is the product $a \times b$?
6. Write a lovers' quarrel in the style of Dr Seuss.
7. Discuss the importance of floating exchange rates to an economic system.
8. Write a football match report in the style of George Orwell.

The answers – written in front of your eyes in seconds – will astonish you.

I will share just two of them. The answers to 1. and 5.

Here is *ChatGPT*'s very elegant answer to my Question 1: 'Write a weather report in the style of a Dr Martin Luther King speech.'

'My fellow Americans, let us look to the heavens and observe the weather that surrounds us. For as we stand here today, the clouds are gathering and the winds are blowing. The temperature, though cool, is a reminder of the resilience and strength that lies within us.

As we move forward, let us not forget that just like the changing seasons, the weather too shall pass. The sun will shine again and the rains will come to nourish the earth.

Let us use this moment to reflect on the power of nature and the majesty of the elements. Let us also remember to be thankful for the shelter that protects us from the elements and to extend a helping hand to those who are less fortunate.

So, my friends, let us embrace this weather, not with fear or trepidation, but with hope and determination. For as we stand together, weathering the storm, we will emerge stronger and more united than ever before.

Thank you, and may God bless the United States of America.'

I can absolutely hear his voice in that answer.

And here is its correct answer to Question 5: 'If a plus b is 8, and the difference between a and b is 3, what is the product $a \times b$?'

'Let a and b be two numbers. Then, we have two equations based on the information given:

$a + b = 8$

$a - b = 3$

Adding the two equations, we get:

$2a = 11$

Dividing both sides by 2, we get:

a = 5.5

To find b, we can substitute the value of a, and use the first equation:

b = 8 - a = 8 - 5.5 = 2.5

Finally, to find the product ab, we multiply a and b:

ab = a × b = 5.5 × 2.5 = 13.75

So, the product of a and b is 13.75.'

How does it work?

AI systems learn and adapt. They are not programmed. They rely on a body of knowledge known as a *corpus*. This is content that is verified and curated through the virtual teaching by thousands of experts, and by regular user feedback loops.

An AI system can read millions of pages a second. It then uses pattern recognition, anomaly detection and predictive analytics to generate an acceptable answer.

In milliseconds (*1,000th of second*), an AI system goes through 4 steps: -

1. **Question analysis** (400 milliseconds).

   The AI will parse the question and understand it as human language. It is not just a key word search, like Google or Alexa.

2. **Hypothesis generation** (500 milliseconds)

   This entails analysing hundreds of millions of documents, sites, journals, structured data (text, numbers) and unstructured data (pdf, video, images).

3. **Evidence scoring** (700 milliseconds).

   Now the AI system will generate some possible answers and score them based on its confidence. At this point, quantity trumps quality.

4. **Answer generation**: final merging and ranking (1,100 milliseconds)

   The final step. The AI will weigh the useful evidence, decide its answer and it will document its level of certainty. If its confidence level is less than 50%, it won't answer. This is a significant step in the evolution of computing. The AI knows what it knows, and knows what it doesn't know.

So within 3 seconds, you'll have an answer.

The *Institute of Chartered Accountants in England & Wales* tried *ChatGPT* on one of its professional exams and it got a very respectable 42%. While below the 55 percent pass mark, this was considered a reasonable attempt. It will get better, and very quickly.

This deep analysis and natural language processing has huge implications for healthcare, medical diagnosis, finance, retail and education – virtually any industry where people are using data to make better decisions.

Let's not be in denial

Prime Minster Rishi Sunak recently described his policy vision for the compulsory study of mathematics up to the age of 18 as 'the closest thing we have to a silver bullet.' The same thing can be said for many of these AI tools — whether it's *ChatGPT* from *OpenAI*, *Bard* from *Google*, *Watson* from *IBM,* or the many others that will undoubtedly appear.

I have always been relaxed about students using *Wikipedia* for their homework. I think it's a constructive and valuable use of online time. At least they're looking in the right places on the web. *Wikipedia* beats Andrew Tate every time.

The economist Milton Friedman was once on a foreign speaking tour. Stuck in traffic due to some roadworks, he asked his hosts why the workers were using shovels, instead of machinery. The answer was that it was a deliberate policy, in order maintain employment levels.

Friedman retorted, 'Then why don't you give them spoons instead of shovels, and create even more jobs?'

In January, 2023, the *New York City Department of Education* restricted access to *ChatGPT* from its public school internet and devices. I believe this to be a misguided, Orwellian, knee-jerk reaction.

In a blinded test, *ChatGPT* was judged to have passed graduate-level exams at the *University of Minnesota* at the level of a C+ student, and at the *Wharton School of the University of Pennsylvania* with a B grade.

We cannot bury our heads in the sand, and should not resist this lightning-speed development. We should cultivate, curate, encourage and savour the leaps that it can give us and our students.

We've been here before

'There is nothing new under the sun.' – *Ecclesiastes*

In the film *Hidden Figures (2016),* the African-American women mathematicians working at NASA were confronted with the oncoming era of computing. An IBM computer is brought in to make computations in seconds – of rocket trajectories, speeds, landing arcs – that previously took humans hours and days to perform.

What happens? The women begin learning the new programming languages, such as COBOL, at night school, and they become the first computer scientists. They were able to improve the computer programs that took the space race into the digital era. The women mathematicians were not replaced — they just moved to a higher order of thinking, and invented a new industry.

Sixty years on, we need to mimic those remarkable and talented women — Kathryn Johnson, Dorothy Vaughn and Mary Jackson, and many others — and carve out a path that combines inspiring magic with gritty realism. Thus, we can make the next generation thrive, and scale the heights of traditional learning, creative ideas and better decisions.

ChatGPT is available to try at: https://openai.com/blog/chatgpt/

28 Redesign

The usual suspects: our first world problems

Common experiences of annoying app designs. Here is a personal hit list for the User Experience (UX) professionals.

1. **'Enter your username.'** We never remember them. They're pointless. Just use my email instead. Preferably not even that. You know who I am. From my face. And my history.
2. **Banking apps Part I.** You are especially terrible. You and credit card apps. No, I don't want to '*go to the website*' to do certain things. The first thing the web site will ask me is to use the app. I've only just come from the app. Make the app do everything the web site does.
3. **Banking apps Part II.** If you don't trust me with just a password, then forget about passwords. Don't ask me for a password and then also text me a 'One Time' password (*OTP*) as well.
4. **Banking apps Part III.** And don't call it a *One Time Password*. It's every single time.
5. **'Text or email me a passcode'**: it means that I need a couple of apps running at once, or two browser windows, or two devices. Just need to rethink the whole thing.

Security is just so tedious. We spend more time trying to get into the apps than doing actual banking on the apps. I'm not a fraudster, and you know this, so stop pretending that you've never met me before, or that someone else is imitating me. I'm not that interesting.

6. **Google maps.** When giving me walking instructions, never, ever say, 'Go East' or 'Go West'. This is completely useless. I'm not Sir Edmund Hillary. I want to know if I should I go left, or go right, or go straight on, or just turn around.

7. **Web sites.** Don't show me a user feedback pop up survey just as soon as I've entered your site. I haven't experienced any *experience* yet to tell you about. Leave me alone. Also *Net Promoter Scores* (NPS) are suspect anyway, because we only use the good ones, and we only send them to people we know will answer favourably.

8. **Multiple log-in options.** This one's a real horrorshow. Confronted with a screen that gives me 4 or 5 different ways to log-in: usually, Google, Apple, Facebook, Outlook and email options. We honestly don't have time to think or worry about this. Just get me in.

9. **Postcode confusion.** Nobody is really sure whether the post code field is *without* spaces or *with* spaces. I have seen every variation of it, and it slows us down.

10. **I am not a robot.** But I'm pretty sure a robot can pass your tests.

    There is an Artificial Intelligence system, *IBM Watson*, that has succeeded in getting through the first few rounds of the *MI5* Intelligence Services online application process. There are very powerful techniques within A.I. systems that have developed to a high degree of sophistication.

Tools like pattern recognition, anomaly detection and predictive analytics.

Also *Decision Trees* are very commonly used in Machine Learning. This is where possible outcomes are listed and a probability of occurrence is attached to them. The outcome value and the probability are multiplied together, to get an 'Expected Value'. It's taught in the A Level Business curriculum, and data scientists use it all the time.

11. **'Are you registered?'** I honestly can't remember. Then when I try to register, it tells me I'm already registered. Tell me that to start with, please. Detect me – patterns of my keyboard behaviour, my fingerprints, face, previous activity, my IP address, my device…anything. I don't mind.

VIII – Work

'There are two types of work: moving things, and telling other people to move things. The first is unpleasant and ill paid. The second is pleasant and well paid.'

— *Bertrand Russell*

29 Chile

'Los 33' and Chile's extreme engineering

'We have cheated death before. We can do it again.'
– *Yonni Barrios, miner*

In 2010, a collapse at the San José mine in Chile trapped 33 men under 700,000 tonnes of rock.

Experts estimated the probability of getting them out alive at less than 1%. Yet, after spending a record 69 days underground, all 33 were rescued.

Exploratory boreholes were drilled to start the rescue. Seventeen days after the accident, a note was found taped to a drill-bit pulled back to the surface: 'Estamos bien en el refugio los 33' ('We are well in the shelter, the 33 of us').

Calm organisation

André Sougarret, led the rescue. A mining engineer with over 20 years of experience, Sougarret managed *El Teniente*, the world's largest underground mine.

At the accident site, Sougarret found chaos. Hundreds of people—the missing men's relatives, the press, first responders from the industry—were flooding in, seeking answers, all adding to the turmoil. He cut through the confusion to establish 'situational awareness' of the complex environment – using tactics employed by air traffic controllers, military leaders, and emergency personnel.

Deep underground, the trapped miners confronted the physical and psychological challenges of survival. Under the calming influence of the shift supervisor, Luis Urzúa, they overcame three days of confusion and conflict to restore order and hope. Threatened by limited food and deteriorating health, the miners adopted a democratic leadership structure. They allocated daily tasks and resources, established living and waste disposal areas, and used the lighting system to simulate day and night.

As they passed the time by sharing stories about their lives, the bonds among them deepened and they began calling themselves *Los 33*.

The rescuers reached out to their networks for new ideas and technologies. Other organizations, such as *NASA*, and *Maptek,* an Australian 3-D mapping software company, volunteered to help.

Miners usually measure results after they finish drilling holes and reach the targeted depth. At the suggestion of the team leaders, the rescue drillers started taking measurements every few hours, abandoning holes that deviated too much and quickly starting over again. The short action-assessment cycles minimised the time and resources spent pursuing fruitless paths and allowed corrections in real time.

Health

The miners were provided with a 5% glucose solution and medicine to prevent stomach ulcers caused by food deprivation. Material sent down the mine took an hour to reach the miners. Delivery of solid food began a few days later. Relatives were permitted to write letters, but were asked to keep them optimistic.

Rescue workers and consultants described the miners as very disciplined – they kept themselves busy and were mentally focused. They confirmed their ability to contribute to the rescue operation. Having a role in their own destiny was important to maintain their motivation and optimism.

Chilean Health Minister Jaime Mañalich stated, 'The situation is very similar to the one experienced by astronauts when they spend months in the International Space Station.'

With few exceptions they were in good medical condition with no long-term physical effects. The US$20 million cost of the rescue was covered by private donations, the mine owners and the government.

Previous geological instability at the mine and a record of safety violations had resulted in a series of fines and accidents, including eight deaths, during the dozen years before this accident.

Three separate drilling rig teams and a dozen corporations from around the world co-operated in completing the heroic liberation. The men were rescued in a specially built capsule, while five million people watched the live video stream.

1st September 2022

30 Teaching IV

Teach like a champion

'Well begun is half done.'
– *Plato, Laws*

The number of teachers leaving the profession in the UK is hitting an all–time high.

33% of qualified teachers leave before their fifth year. 39% by the tenth year. The staff turnover is both a significant challenge – lost corporate knowledge and institutional capability, but it is also source of valuable regeneration – rather like crop rotation, burning down the dead wood and introducing energetic and invigorating new soil agents.

In response, the *Department for Education* has developed an *Early Career Framework (ECF)*, to support newly qualified teachers in their first two years in the classroom. At first sight, and after a year of experiencing it, it just feels like more paperwork, with negligible fruits and imperceptible utility.

High Expectations is one of the *Teacher Standards** and is core to school culture. This is a belief in the academic potential of all pupils through the language we use, fostering a positive culture of respect and trust in the classroom allowing students to feel safe to make mistakes as part of learning within a challenging curriculum.

Manage Behaviour Effectively, is another standard. This is to develop a positive and predictable environment for pupils, through a supportive classroom. This is supported by establishing effective rituals, routines and expectations with students that build trusting relationships. All this is needed to motivate pupils to master their subject and take on the challenges of their long-term journey.

Warm

'*Warm*' provides the language used to foster mutual respect and a belief that (a) the student can achieve great things academically and personally in their time at school, and (b) that the student believes the teacher is genuine through their actions and interactions with that student.

If a student knows you will, without doubt, follow up on behaviour issues, you establish a reputation quickly.

Peacekeepers in the military say it's easier to get people on–side if you've established a good relationship. Using 'forced compliance' and a behaviour management system requires far more effort, and meets more resistance.

Strict

Tending to the 'broken windows'. This is where the high expectations play out. By 'sweating the small stuff', the tone is set for the expectations you have for students.

Not having a pen or pencil can be part of a wider pastoral picture, and an early sign of issues. Off–task behaviour can be dealt with by using low impact interventions, such as standing near a student who is off task, tapping the desk, or possibly visual signals that do not break the flow of teaching. These are all learned and developed in the classroom.

Strict is not shouting like a Sergeant Major at students, 'flattening the grass', or being oppressive. *Strict* relies on students understanding that schools are communities within their own community, in the place where they live. The Army takes people from all backgrounds, and gives them a clear shared sense of belonging to something. In schools the goal is the same. By feeling a sense of belonging in their school community, students take pride in it and in themselves. *Strict* isn't judgemental, *strict* is nurturing and guiding. It is helping form children into adults, and knowing that this will all come with mistakes.

Humour and humility

Like all relationships, humour plays a part in building trust.

Keeping behavioural expectations high, even on the small things, means that the big things rarely happen. Calmness, consistency, following policy – it supports everyone with 'getting it right'.

* - The eight *Teacher Standards* are: *High Expectations, Outcomes, Subject Knowledge, Planning, Adaptation, Assessment, Behaviour,* and *Wider Professional Responsibilities.*

('*Teaching I, II and III*' appear in the book *Angels of Morphia*, 2022)

1ˢᵗ December 2022

31 Teaching V

Cover lessons: Also known as 'Fake it till you make it'. Or, 'How to lose all your new friends in 600 words.'

Sometimes, we are assigned to cover other teachers' lessons if they're not in, and when we have a free period.

Often, it's actually quite good fun. And I always want to actually teach, rather than just hand out the work that's been set. (I still have rose-tinted glasses on. Steaming up, but still on.)

Most of what follows is true.

The easiest lessons to cover ...

Maths — Always well planned, always low maintenance. Do the worksheets. Be quiet. Then use your green pens to mark your neighbour's work.

English — Write a newspaper article about a local crime. Then we'll read two of them out to the class. (*A student hand goes up.*) Yes, of course it can be about the murder of your English teacher. Actually, it *must* be about the murder of your English teacher. In fact, take it easy for an hour, I'll write this one for you.

History — Draw some chopped-off heads celebrating the Peasants' Revolt of 1381. Use red. Make a poster encouraging other peasants to join the revolt. This helps train you for your left-wing adulthood. Lessons from history – it's always 'us and them.'

Geography — Green crayons essential.

I do have one fact about Geography, that I shared with a class once.

Sinuosity means the twisty-ness of a river. First, measure this bendy distance of a river by following its meandering stream. Then, measure the direct distance, as the crow flies. If you divide the former by the latter, you get an incredible result.

For example, the river Thames starts in Kemble, Gloucestershire and then eventually flows into the North Sea in Essex. Its winding length is 346km. Its direct, 'crow flies' length is 110km.

So, 346km divided by 110km, is 3.14. Which is the value of *Pi* (π). Boom. True for all rivers.

RE teachers call this *Intelligent Design*. Science and geography teachers would then claim that it's not the same for all rivers. Which is why science and geography teachers never get invited to the pub.

RE — I once covered a lesson on Judaism, and the afterlife. On the list of people who do not get to heaven, it said: *Epicureans*. I know my Greek philosophy, so I taught the class about Epicurus and his followers.

Epicureans believed that the universe was composed of atoms. (*Yep, they were right. Clever, those Greeks.*). They also believed that gods existed, but that they were not interested in human affairs and did not play an active role in the world. Epicureans believed that the highest goal in life was seeking pleasure.

In contrast, the Jewish tradition teaches that human beings have a purpose beyond seeking pleasure, and that we have ethical obligations to our fellow human beings. Judaism viewed Epicureanism as a threat, promoting hedonism and moral relativism. Both of which are essential ingredients in any decent school trip. Especially the overseas ones.

Art — That's good. That's nice. That's amazing. Clean up now.

The hardest lessons to cover ...

PE — Honestly wouldn't know where to start, or how to stand, or what to say.

Drama — Oh jeez. Do you really need to take your shoes off? OK, then break up into groups of four, and find a space and then say stuff to each other. The louder the better.

Modern Foreign Languages — No, I can't help you. Not because I don't want to, but because I can't. Anyway, you should be learning Chinese and Arabic and Russian. Who really needs French these days? We've gone beyond the world of day trips to Boulogne. You'll all be working for Chinese companies one day.

Science — Thankfully, nobody does experiments anymore, so there's no gas or glass tubes to worry about. Read the textbook and answer these questions. One of the answers is usually Magnesium.

27th April 2023

32 Cobalt

Our techno-feudalism

Rubber and Cobalt

The Democratic Republic of Congo (DRC) has been *blessed* with munificent natural abundance. And the great economic powers — corporations — are in deep to extract the loot. I'm not even talking about tin, tungsten, tantalum and gold (known as 3TG), or diamonds.

In the 1880s it was rubber. Today, it's cobalt. Result: the same. The top 2% get our cars, modern goods and comforts. The 98% look on. They dig and distribute, and lift and shift, and die for the cause of our 'renewable', gadget-driven lifestyles.

Cobalt based blue pigments have been used since ancient times for jewellery and paints. Today, cobalt is used for rechargeable batteries for mobile phones, laptops, tablets and computers. Increasingly, it is being used for the batteries of Electric Vehicles (EV's).

Siddharth Kara at Harvard University is the world's foremost authority on modern slave labour and human trafficking. He has studied it in the field for 23 years, across 50 countries.

What he saw in the Congo, 'was like going back in time. Imagine what mining was like 300 or 400 year ago.'

Two car revolutions tell the story of enforced slave labour.

Congo, 1880s: King Leopold of Belgium took control of the Congo in 1885. Benz invents the car. Dunlop invents the rubber tyre, in 1888. The Congo had the largest rubber tree forests in the world. Leopold employed mercenary armies to enslave the local population and extract the rubber to make tyres.

Joseph Conrad saw all this in 1890. This is what inspired his novel *Heart of Darkness*.

Congo, 2022: Now we have the second car revolution – EV's. The DRC sits on more cobalt than the rest of the planet combined. Some mines have 15,000 miners digging with simple picks, by hand, without protective equipment, in flip-flops, and breathing in the toxins. Cobalt is poisonous before it's refined.

Options

Many things could be done to improve the working and living conditions of hundreds of thousands of people. The cost of taking these measures is a rounding error on the balance sheet of major technology corporations. Less than a day's revenue.

Without pausing for breath ... the following would help pave the way for more tolerable working conditions: Personal Protective Equipment; Reasonable wages: so that workers do not need to bring their children to work, just to survive; Fewer working hours; Schools; Health clinics; Electrification; Water; Sanitation.

The supply chain runs deep, with many firms protected by armed militias and mobile commando units. 15 of the largest 19 cobalt mines in the Congo are run by *Chinese mining companies*. ('Chinese companies' means the Chinese government.)

Who is responsible for taking action? There are so many complex integrated levels between a toxic pit in the Congo, and the shiny showrooms of New York, London and Beijing.

The big technology and EV companies say the battery manufacturers should fix it. The battery companies say the cobalt refineries should take care of it. The refineries look at the mining companies. The mining companies say the Congolese government are accountable. Eventually, the last finger is pointed at the kid, caked in filth, down the pit.

Kara is willing to take any tech CEOs down to the bottom of their cobalt supply chain, and work to fix this problem. These companies have geniuses who have revolutionised our lives. 'Solving *dignity* is a simpler proposition to the problems they solve every day', says Kara.

Currently, newer cobalt recycling innovations do not produce sufficient grade cobalt to put back into an EV battery. Cobalt-free batteries are being worked on as we speak.

6th April 2023

IX – Books

'**Philosophy,** *noun*. A route of many roads, leading from nowhere to nothing.'

– Ambrose Bierce, The Enlarged Devil's Dictionary

33 Salman

The spell of stories

Salman Rushdie's book '*Joseph Anton*' is a memoir of his years under the protection of Special Branch, after the 1989 *fatwa* from Iran's Ayatollah Khomeini, sanctioning his murder for writing an allegedly profane book. *The Satanic Verses* is a spirited novel about migration, exile, belonging, and tradition, and included playful sections on the prophet Mohamed. Without having read the book, many Muslims condemned it.

Rushdie went into hiding and was afforded protection from the UK state. As Christopher Hitchens once eloquently said, 'Can you think of a better way to spend our money, than on the defence of free expression?' That Special Branch protection lasted 13 years, until 2002, when the security services deemed the threat level to have fallen sufficiently.

Joseph Anton was the pseudonym that he chose in order to continue with 'normal' life (bank accounts, contracts) – combining the first names of two writers that he admired, Conrad and Chekhov.

We've Got Simple, We've Got Complicated

A dinner with friends. What could possibly go wrong?

'Harold Pinter and Antonia Fraser came to dinner at The Bishop's Avenue. Robert McCrum, a little slower than he used to be, with a sweet, vague smile on his face, and his wife, Sarah Lyall, were the other guests, and when Harold discovered that Robert worked for the *Observer*, with which he had some unmemorable political quarrel, and that Sarah worked for the hated, because American, *New York Times*, he launched into one of his loudest, longest, least attractive bouts of Pintering.

Dear Harold,

You know my admiration for you and, I hope, that I value our friendship highly; but I can't let the events of last night pass unremarked upon. Robert, a good man bravely fighting back from a stroke, is simply not able to speak and argue as freely as he once did, and retreated under your assault into a miserable silence. Sarah, whom I like very much, was almost reduced to tears and, worse, amazed to find herself in the position of defending US Zionism-imperialism as embodied by the New York Times. Elizabeth and I both felt that our hospitality had been abused and our evening ruined. The grand slam, in fact. I can't help saying that I mind very much about all this. It happens all the time, and as your friend I must ask you to STOP IT. On Cuba, on East Timor, on so many issues you are much more right than wrong, but these tirades - when you appear to assume that others have failed to notice the offences that outrage you - are just plain tiresome. I think you owe us all an apology.

With much love, Salman

Dear Salman,

Your letter was very painful for me to read but I am grateful to you for it. You write as a true friend. What you say is absolutely true and in this case the truth is bitter. There is no justification for my behaviour and I have no defence. I can only say this: I hear myself bullying and boring but it's like a St Vitus's dance, a fever, an appalling sickening - and of course drunken - descent into incoherence and insult. Lamentable. Your letter was really a whip of iced water and has had a great effect on me. I have to believe it's not too late for me to grow up. I do send heartfelt apologies to you and Elizabeth. I care for you both so much. I have written to the McCrums.

With my love, Harold

Dear Harold,

Thank you for your letter. Water under the bridge. We love you very much.

Salman'

6th October 2022

34 Boxer

Boxer the cart-horse is introduced on page one of George Orwell's *Animal Farm*.

'Boxer was an enormous beast ... and as strong as any two ordinary horses put together. He was universally respected for his steadiness of character and tremendous powers of work.'

He fights bravely against the humans. He is loyal and caring. Unfortunately, the pigs take advantage of this and work him until he collapses. They sell him to the slaughterhouse so that they can buy more whisky. Whenever something goes wrong, he blames himself and vows to work even harder.

His favourite sayings are 'Napoleon is always right' and 'I will work harder'. He is the strongest animal and could easily fight off the pigs and dogs. He never does though, as he is too used to taking orders.

Boxer believes everything that Napoleon (*Stalin*) tells him. The language is simple and reflects Boxer's naivety; he does nothing when conditions get worse.

Orwell's description of Boxer is emotive and inspirational: 'To see him toiling up the slope inch by inch, his breath coming fast, the tips of his hoofs clawing at the ground, and his great sides matted with sweat, filled everyone with admiration.'

He never complains or lacks motivation. Even though he is described as dim, he takes the initiative when it comes to work: 'He had made arrangements with the cockerel to call him three-quarters of an hour earlier in the morning instead of half an hour.'

Real life model

Boxer is based on a real coal miner named Alexey Stakhanov who was famous for working hard to exceed his allocated quota of coal production. All for the cause of 'Mother Russia'. Joseph Stalin built a cult of personality around him that rewarded workers who showed a similar heroic dedication to production and efficiency. Boxer supported Napoleon and also was very loyal to his kind. Unlike Boxer, Stakhanov was allowed to retire and ultimately outlived Stalin.

Boxer represents the exploited workers of Russia under Tsar Nicholas II, who ruled from 1894 until his expulsion in 1917. The workers never earned enough for food or accommodation. The Revolution of 1917 sought to address this, but only led to betrayal, more hardship and starvation under the cruel rule of Stalin.

English cartoonist David Low used a cart horse as a symbol for the Trades Union Congress in cartoons in the 1930s and 40s, years before Orwell began to write *Animal Farm*.

Like a lot of the other animals, except the pigs, Boxer lacks an education. Orwell uses this to show that without the benefit of learning, he cannot express himself to speak out against the pigs: 'several times he tried to marshal his thoughts; but he couldn't think of anything to say.'

Boxer fights in the Battle of the Cowshed and the Battle of the Windmill. When he collapses from overwork, the pigs say they have sent him to a veterinarian, when they have sent him instead to the knacker's yard.

The other animals concoct a sentimental tale of the death of Boxer, saying that he was given the best medical care possible, paid for by the 'compassionate' Napoleon. Boxer's death is turned into a day in his honour. Squealer says that his sayings, 'Comrade Napoleon is always right' and 'I will work harder!' should live on in all animals – another excuse to make them work even harder. As head of propaganda, Squealer ensures that small lies lead to bigger lies.

Boxer's strength keeps Animal Farm together: the animals trusted him to keep their spirits high during the long, hard and laborious winters.

2nd February 2023

35 Liz

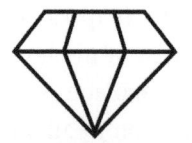

Book review: 'Elizabeth Taylor's Kiss – And Other Brushes with Hollywood', by David Wood

'Was this the face that launch'd a thousand ships,
And burnt the topless towers of Ilium –
Sweet Helen, make me immortal with a kiss.'
– *Christopher Marlowe, Dr Faustus*

If you were to draw a Venn diagram of the marriages of Richard Burton and Elizabeth Taylor, you'd have 2 in the common / conjoined area, 3 in the Burton only and 6 in the Taylor only areas.

Their two marriages to each other were from 1964 to 1974, and then again from 1975 to 1976. Not much more need be said. Fiery, red-blooded, inebriated, vinous, overweening and vainglorious. They acted in 11 films together. None of which are much watched now.

This book is highly readable and jaunts along merrily. David Wood, the author, has a nice conversational style, that makes reading this book like drinking water. Pleasant.

I am sure that nobody under the age of 35 will have heard of Elizabeth Taylor. She is to this generation what Norma Desmond was to previous generations: a symbol of a bygone era, a faded legend and with forgotten notoriety. Still, the star shone brightly. Anyone aged between 35 and 60 will have heard of her, but never seen any of her films.

Wood studied English at Worcester College Oxford in the 1960s. He was more interested in theatrical adventures at the *Oxford University Dramatic Society.* So much so that his long-suffering tutor, Sir Christopher Ricks, had become used to late essays and missed tutorials.

He was participating as a student actor in Christopher Marlowe's *Dr Faustus,* when it was announced that Hollywood stars Richard Burton and Elizabeth Taylor would come to participate in it. He relayed this news to Professor Ricks who duly noted that it was too unique an opportunity to pass up, but suggested that Wood should work extra hard for the rest of the term: 'You never know what long-term life will be like, and it would be as well for you to have a respectable degree. So do a lot of work. I've spoken to the Provost, and he concurs.'

And so it was, the Burtons arrived in a chauffeur driven, green Rolls-Royce, and slotted into the play seamlessly. They'd done their homework. In the pub one day, with her entourage and adoring student actors, Taylor noticed Wood's tatty and frayed jumper, and brought two of Burton's for him the next day.

All this was a long way from their Hollywood lifestyles. And far away from Burton's youth. Growing up in South Wales, all the male members of his family were coal miners. Burton talked about the famous coal seam, called the *Great Atlantic Fault.* It starts in northern Spain, in Basque country, and it goes under the Bay of Biscay and comes up in South Wales, and then it goes under the Atlantic and comes up in

Pennsylvania, so that if you took a Basque miner, or a Welsh miner, or a Pennsylvanian miner, and if you could blindfold them and transport them – they'd know the coalface as soon as they saw it. A gorgeous black, shining ribbon of coal. It was this romanticism that Burton brought to his acting and his famous baritone voice.

The 'other brushes' in the book involve acting in a play with Shelley Winters (who was the American one in *Alfie)*, and alongside Malcolm McDowell, Christopher Plummer, Anthony Perkins and Roger Moore in very forgettable films, which furnish the author with equally forgettable anecdotes. Anthony Perkins was friendly and accomplished at word games.

15th September 2022

X – Places

'The real voyage of discovery consists not in seeking new landscapes, but in having new eyes.'

– Marcel Proust

36 Jurisdictions

Shopping for policy in 'High Performing Jurisdictions'

Comparisons in educational outcomes between countries have been carried out for decades.

The league tables are published, and the nations at the top become labelled as *High Performing Jurisdictions* ('HPJs'). HPJs are the legal, national or geographic entities that lead the world in educational attainment.

The lagging countries seek to emulate the practices of HPJs. The main index that has become the prominent measure is *PISA (Programme for International Student Assessment)*.

The countries/jurisdictions that perform consistently at the top of these league tables: Singapore, Finland, China, South Korea, Japan, Israel, Switzerland, Hong Kong, The Netherlands and Estonia, are also competing well against the USA and the UK in the new economies of digital technology, online marketplaces and renewable energy. Israel is an important hub for the latest developments in Artificial Intelligence.

All this has led to a 'what works best' fetishism, that meant huge costs were spent visiting 'high performing' locations to bring back the mythical secret *elixir* from which all could benefit.

Comparisons

Benchmarking is a useful tool in business. Annual reports show corporate pay comparisons against *equivalent peer group* companies. Petrochemical manufacturers and refineries use a standard index (the *Solomon score*) to compare production efficiency, operational performance, product yields, and environmental emission controls. Price comparisons between the major supermarket chains and fuel stations happens in real-time, with new prices automatically updated in *Point-of-Sale* systems.

It can be exciting to want to judiciously choose the best teaching ideas from so-called 'best practices', and to concoct a heady brew of pedagogical gold that's then promoted as 'fit for everyone'. However, how can one compare Singapore, with its 5m population and 350 schools, with the United Kingdom's 68m people and 24,000 schools?

I am especially interested in this subject, as I worked with global corporations for many years, implementing new ways of working and new systems. These were typically standard design templates that we would roll out across many countries.

People in developing countries (Angola, Vietnam, Ghana, South Africa) were typically a joy to work with. Eager, interested, engaged, committed, kind and able to see the big picture. The people in developed countries (United Kingdom, The Netherlands, USA) however, had an impatient and cynical attitude, sceptical of change, and confident in their long-established ways of working.

But local practices were often just enshrined habits, and it was much easier for them to adjust and adopt the global model, rather than change the template itself. This saved millions of pounds and enabled workers to transfer between countries more easily and work in a common way. It gave employees in developing countries inspiration and opportunity to apply for jobs in globally diverse locations, and progress their careers.

Career

Lessons from Finland (one of the top HPJs) are that a broader science-based education and the requirement to have a master's degree, lead to high calibre teachers. Add to this, the pleasant school environments and the generally higher standing and respect in society for teaching, means that Finnish teachers stay in their chosen careers throughout their whole life (*OECD, 2018*). They are also paid much better than in other countries. Only 1 in 10 applicants in Finland are accepted into teaching, such are the rigours of the selection process. In some countries teaching is 'one of the top three career choices' (*McKinsey*).

The purpose of education is more than merely preparing young minds to become economic beings. Citizenship, equity, curiosity, engagement, compassion, empathy, physical and mental health are also shaping the curriculum.

25th August 2022

37 Iraq

'Stuff Happens': Iraq in 2003 – 2004

Ray Jennings is a politics lecturer at Georgetown University. He visited Iraq in 2003, and was in the Green Zone at the former presidential palace, in Baghdad, where the *Coalition Provisional Authority* (CPA) had set up its compound.

He bumped into one of his graduates, and asked her what she was doing.

'I can't believe my luck. I'm being asked to do the traffic plan for city.'

She had no training in municipal planning.

The CPA was set up to begin post-war operations in Iraq. Virtually nobody spoke Arabic in the CPA; maybe five out of the 70 officials.

Paul Bremer was the Presidential envoy who led the CPA. He made two fateful policy decisions.

CPA Order Number 1: De-Ba'athification. This was to ensure that the structure and influence of the Ba'ath Party, which had ruled Iraq under Saddam Hussein, was eliminated.

This purged 50,000 members of the Ba'ath Party – meaning permanent unemployment. The order crippled Iraq's government, educational system and economy. Most joined the party just to survive under Saddam's regime.

People were kicked out of their jobs, even though they were just professionals. Engineers, directors, the technocrats, the intelligentsia, the elementary school librarian. Being conquered and then not being able to support your family was humiliating.

CPA Order Number 2: Disbanding the Iraqi Military and the Intelligence services. Previously the most important institutions in Iraq.

Overnight, Bremer's order rendered unemployed, and thereby infuriated, half a million armed men. Equivalent to firing all the NHS staff in the UK. And so these men, rather than helping to prevent an insurgency, instead created one.

Millions of people depended on army incomes. It was no surprise that they turned to joining the insurgency, to feed their families, and to regain some pride.

Iraq contained 70 large weapons storage depots and many more unguarded ammunition dumps. There were not enough American troops to secure them. They were looted and the arms were used against the Americans.

American Colonel Paul Hughes, could not believe what was happening. He had spent months building relationships with senior Iraqi army officers. The army was standing there, waiting for an overture, that someone would come to them and say, 'This is the plan. And you are integral to that plan. And we need you.' No-one ever did that.

One of the Iraqi officers said to Hughes, 'Colonel Paul, I can have 10,000 military policemen for you next week. You just tell me.' Hughes took that to Bremer and nothing was done with it. Bremer issued the disbanding order. Those men could have kept the peace.

Even more remarkable than the decision to disband the army, was *how* that decision was made – secretly, over a single week, by four men in Washington DC: Donald Rumsfeld, Paul Wolfowitz, Dick Cheney, and Walter Slocombe (Under Secretary for Defence, responsible for Iraq's post war military). It was done *without* consulting the US military commanders in Iraq, the Joint Chiefs of Staff, the State Department, the CIA, the National Security Council ... or even the President of the United States.

The State department had prepared a list of twenty sites that needed to be protected – historical, cultural, artistic, religious, strategic.

Number one on the list was the *Iraq National Museum*. It contained artefacts from the earliest human civilisations. 7,000 years of historical treasures. It was never protected, and was looted. *Iraq's National Library and Archives* containing thousands of ancient manuscripts was burnt down.

The oil ministry was the only major facility protected by the U.S. Military.

24th March 2023

38 Cyprus

Εσσι'έναν άστρον
Τζι'έν μιτσίν
Με'στους εφτά πλανήτες.

'There's this tiny star,
Among the seven planets.'

– Traditional

In August 2022, I crossed a pseudo-'border' at Deryneia, and travelled into the illegally occupied territory of northern Cyprus for one day.

Eight months earlier, a Turkish Cypriot friend and I were talking at work. He said that when I was next in Cyprus I should go across the 'border' and visit the north.

I said, 'Why would I want to do that?'

He said, 'I'll take you to St Andreas monastery.'

That stopped me in my tracks.

Apart from the fulfilling and uplifting time at the monastery, at the Eastern tip of the island, I found the trip to be a bittersweet experience. I was in the company of a friend, and I enjoyed his hospitality. But I was angered at the injustice of legitimate homeowners being prevented from living in their houses, by an occupying force, and strangers transported in from mainland Turkey.

Father Zacharias

When we arrived at Apostolos Andreas monastery, in the early evening, the priest/monk was conducting the Vespers service.

I walked around and took some pictures. The site is being maintained, re-built and developed using *UN* and *Church of Cyprus* funding.

After Vespers, I entered the church sanctuary, and greeted the priest.

Me:	(*In Greek*) How long have you been here, Father?
Father Zacharias:	Sixty years.
Me:	(*amazed*) You've been here sixty years!
FZ:	Since July 1962. Until today. (*Prepares a wick, to be lit in a hanging lantern.*) There's nobody here. I'm on my own.
Me:	Do you have any chanters?
FZ:	I toil alone. Unless any happen to drop in, by chance. *(Handing me a lit candle).* Light this lantern. *(I do so.)* Your grace, Apostle Andreas. *(Then to me)* Whatever you desire.

Economics

I asked my friend about the situation within the Turkish Cypriot community. What sustains them? What drives the economy of the occupied northern area? What are the main industries and jobs?

His answer shocked me.

Without hesitation, he said: 'Casinos, prostitution, drugs. And handouts from Turkey.'

I was expecting the usual Mediterranean answer: agriculture and tourism.

He could have added human trafficking, for which the Turkish occupied zone is becoming infamous, with an established passage from the 'Stans' – the former Soviet republics.

I felt sick. This region was developing fast in the early 1970s. It's now mostly ghost towns. Even the inhabited villages had no vibrancy, no civic presence, no community feeling. Nobody was sitting on their verandas, as they normally do in Cyprus. It's as if the inhabitants were ashamed to be there.

There is also an unfortunate habit of some Greek Cypriots, to go across to the north to fill their cars with cheaper fuel, and to visit casinos and nightclubs. The traffic in the other direction, by contrast, is Turkish Cypriots coming to the south for legitimate work. The Republic of Cyprus is, after all, a member of the European Union.

Spending

The next day, back in the south, I went to dinner with siblings and cousins. I took some heat for my trip, and was questioned, quite rightly. My beloved cousin, Sophia, said she would never go north in the present circumstances. She could not stomach being asked for her ID card in order to 'cross over' – to travel *on her own land*. Very fair point. Sophia's brothers Demetri and Yianno were especially vociferous in their insults. I can still picture them now, shaking their heads, in unison, at me.

I gave a transparent account of my day's spending! Had I contributed to their economy?

€75. That's €5 for coffees (my friend had paid for the fish meze); €20 for fridge magnets at Apostolos Andreas, as gifts. And I gave €50 into the hand of Father Zacharias.

Our island's true borders extend to the sea.

Our borders are at Kyrenia.

23rd February 2023

XI – Society

'I'm with you in Rockland in my dreams you walk dripping from a sea-journey on the highway across America in tears to the door of my cottage in the Western night.'

– *Allen Ginsberg, 'Howl'*

39 Eichmann

Next year in Jerusalem: Hunting Nazis, Mossad style

Adolf Eichmann (1906 – 1962) was a German-Austrian Obersturmbannführer (Senior Assault-Unit Leader) in the Schutzstaffel (SS), the 'Protection Squadron' paramilitary organisation in Nazi Germany, and one of the organisers of the Holocaust. He was tasked with the logistics for the mass deportation of millions of Jews to ghettos and extermination camps in Nazi-occupied Eastern Europe.

Eichmann escaped from post-war Germany and went into hiding in Argentina. In 1960, Israel's secret service, The Mossad, sent an eight-man team to find him. Eichmann was captured on 11 May 1960 and subsequently found guilty of war crimes in Jerusalem. He was executed by hanging in 1962.

Argentina had a history of turning down extradition requests for Nazi criminals, so Israeli Prime Minister David Ben-Gurion decided that Eichmann should be captured and brought to Israel for trial. Eichmann was interrogated daily, whilst awaiting trial. The transcripts totalled 3,500 pages.

Trial

Eichmann appeared before Jerusalem's Central Court on 11 April 1961. Under the 1950 *Nazi and Nazi Collaborators (Punishment) Law*, he was indicted on 15 criminal charges, including crimes against humanity, war crimes, crimes against the Jewish people, and membership in a criminal organisation. The trial was presided over by three judges: Moshe Landau, Benjamin Halevy and Yitzhak Raveh.

Eichmann sat inside a bulletproof glass booth. Videotape of the trial was flown daily to the United States for broadcast the following day. The prosecution case was presented over 56 days, with hundreds of documents and 112 witnesses, many of them Holocaust survivors.

Some of the evidence for the defence involved depositions by leading Nazis. The defence team demanded that they were brought to Israel. This was denied by the Attorney General, Gideon Hausner, saying that he would arrest any war criminals who entered Israel.

The prosecution proved that Eichmann had visited Chełmno extermination camp, Auschwitz, and Minsk, and therefore was aware that the deportees were being killed. In his testimony, Eichmann insisted he followed orders, and was bound by an oath of loyalty to Hitler — the same defence that other Nazis used in the 1945–1946 Nuremberg trials.

The verdict was read on 12 December 1961. Eichmann was convicted on all 15 counts.

He was responsible for the dreadful conditions onboard the deportation trains and for obtaining Jews to fill those trains. In addition, he was convicted for crimes against Poles, Slovenes and Gypsies. On 15 December 1961, Eichmann was sentenced to death by hanging.

Appeals and execution

Eichmann's defence team appealed the verdict to the Israeli Supreme Court and to Israeli President Yitzhak Ben-Zvi for clemency. The appeal for clemency was denied.

Eichmann was hanged at a prison in Ramla, 1 June 1962. His last words were, 'Long live Germany. Long live Argentina. Long live Austria. These are the three countries with which I have been most connected and which I will not forget. I greet my wife, my family and my friends. I am ready. We'll meet again soon, as is the fate of all men. I die believing in God.'

Eichmann's body was cremated, and his ashes scattered in the Mediterranean Sea, outside Israeli territorial waters, by a Navy patrol boat.

Aftermath

The trial and the surrounding media coverage sparked renewed interest in wartime events, resulting in the publication of memoirs and scholarly works.

Eichmann's son Ricardo Eichmann was not resentful toward Israel for executing his father. He said that the 'following orders' argument does not excuse his father's actions. Ricardo was a professor of archaeology at the German Archaeological Institute.

14th July 2022

40 Eichmann II

The 'banality of evil'

Claude Lanzmann (Film director): *Why do you smile all the time?*

Mordechai Podchlebnik (Holocaust survivor): *Sometimes you smile, sometimes you cry. And if you're alive, it's better to smile.'*

– Shoah, 1985

The book *'Eichmann in Jerusalem'* is a truly riveting read. It was written by political philosopher Hannah Arendt in 1963.

Arendt, a Jew who fled Germany during Adolf Hitler's rise to power, reported on the trial of Nazi Adolf Eichmann for *The New Yorker* magazine.

Arendt's book introduced the notorious phrase *'the banality of evil'*. It refers to Eichmann displaying neither guilt for his actions nor hatred for those trying him. He claimed he bore no responsibility because he was 'doing his job, and obeyed the law.'

Before his trial, the Israeli government sent no fewer than six psychologists to examine Eichmann. They found no trace of mental illness, and no personality disorders. One doctor remarked that his attitude towards people, especially family and friends, was 'highly desirable'. Another remarked that the only unusual trait Eichmann displayed was being 'more normal in his habits and speech than the average person.'

Eichmann stated in court that he tried to abide by Immanuel Kant's *categorical imperative*: 'Act only according to that rule as if it were universal law.' Arendt argues that Eichmann had taken the wrong lesson from Kant: Eichmann had not recognised the 'golden rule', but had understood only the concept of one's actions coinciding with general law.

Eichmann attempted to follow the spirit of the laws he carried out, as if the legislator himself would approve. In Kant's categorical imperative, the legislator is the moral self, and all people are legislators; in Eichmann's version, the legislator was Hitler. Arendt claims that he had ceased to live according to Kantian principles, and he knew it, and he had consoled himself with the thought that he no longer 'was master of his own deeds,' and was unable 'to change anything'.

Eichmann's inability to think for himself was exemplified by his use of 'stock phrases and clichés'. He demonstrated poor communication skills through his constant use of 'officialese' (*Amtssprache)* and euphemistic *Sprachregelung* (conventions of speech) that made implementation of Hitler's policies 'somehow palatable.' Arendt concluded that he showed 'no fanatical anti-Semitism of any kind.' This angered her friends and critics alike.

Eichmann was a 'joiner' his entire life. He constantly joined organisations in order to define himself, and had difficulty thinking for himself without doing so. As a youth, he belonged to the YMCA. In 1933, he failed when trying to join the Schlaraffia (an organization similar to Freemasonry), at which point a friend (and future war criminal) Ernst Kaltenbrunner encouraged him to join the SS.

At the end of the war, Eichmann was distressed that he'd have to live without being a member of something: 'I would have a leaderless life, with no directives, no orders, no pertinent ordinances to consult — a life never known before, now lay ahead of me.'

Eichmann witnessed the rank-and-file of the German civil service endorse Reinhard Heydrich's programme for the Final Solution of the Jewish question in Europe (German: *die Endlösung der Judenfrage*). As 'respectable society' endorsed mass murder, Eichmann felt his moral responsibility was relaxed, 'like Pontius Pilate.'

Arendt discredits the idea that Nazi criminals were psychopathic and different from 'normal' people. Many concluded that situations such as the Holocaust can make ordinary people commit enormous crimes with the right incentives. But Arendt insisted that moral choice remains even under totalitarianism. This choice has consequences even when the chooser is politically powerless.

28th July 2022

41 Eichmann III

Resistance

Denmark

The story of Danish resistance to Nazi occupation is one that Hannah Arendt, the distinguished political philosopher, recommends as required reading in political science for all students who wish to learn something about the enormous power potential inherent in non-violent action. And in resistance to a formidable opponent who has vastly superior firepower and methods of violence.

It was not just that the people of Denmark refused to assist in implementing the Final Solution, as the peoples of so many other conquered nations had been persuaded to do (or had been eager to do) — but also, that when the Reich cracked down and decided to do the job itself it found that its own personnel in Denmark had been infected by this and were unable to overcome their human aversion with the appropriate ruthlessness, as their peers in more cooperative areas had.

Like Denmark, also Sweden, Italy, and Bulgaria proved to be nearly immune to anti-Semitism, but only the Danes dared speak out on the subject to their German masters. Italy and Bulgaria sabotaged German orders and indulged in a complicated game of double-dealing and double-crossing, saving their Jews by a tour de force of sheer ingenuity, but they never contested the policy as such.

That was totally different from what the Danes did. When the Germans approached them rather cautiously about introducing the yellow badge, they were simply told that the King would be the first to wear it, and the Danish government officials were careful to point out that anti-Jewish measures of any sort would cause their own immediate resignation.

The Germans did not succeed in introducing the important distinction between native Danes of Jewish origin, the German Jewish refugees who had found asylum in the country prior to the war, and who now had been declared stateless by the German government.

This refusal must have surprised the Germans, since it appeared so 'illogical' for a government to protect people to whom it had categorically denied naturalisation and even permission to work. The Danes explained to the German officials that because the stateless refugees were no longer German citizens, the Nazis could not claim them without Danish assent. This is a rare case where being stateless was actually an asset.

You must hang

Arendt ended her book, *Eichmann in Jerusalem*, by chillingly addressing Eichmann directly: 'Just as you supported and carried out a policy of not wanting to share the earth with the Jewish people and the people of a number of other nations — as though you and your superiors had any right to determine who should and who should not inhabit the world — we find that no one can be expected to want to share the earth with you. This is the reason, and the only reason, you must hang.'

After *Eichmann in Jerusalem* was published in 1963, controversy followed Hannah Arendt for many years. In his 2006 book, *Becoming Eichmann: Rethinking the Life, Crimes and Trial of a 'Desk Murderer'*, Holocaust researcher David Cesarani questioned Arendt's portrait of Eichmann. Cesarani alleges that Arendt's claims stand on weak foundations – that Eichmann's motives were 'banal' and non-ideological and that he had abdicated his autonomy of choice by obeying Hitler's orders.

This is a recurrent criticism of Arendt. However, nowhere in her work does she deny that Eichmann was an anti-Semite. Also, she also did not claim that Eichmann was simply following orders, but rather that he had internalised the clichés of the Nazi regime.

11th August 2022

42 Water

Neo-Hydro

'The greatest however, is water'
Ἄριστον μὲν ὕδωρ
– *Pindar*

The infrastructure of the UK's water industry dates back to the Victorian era. Pipes, pumps, sewers. Despite adding newer assets, such as pumping stations, desalination plants, storage reservoirs and tanks, the water companies have found it hard to manage their physical and digital assets, combined with the challenges of a distributed workforce that operates in all weathers.

The sector is included within the UK's Critical National Infrastructure (CNI) – the high importance, high risk, high resilience services that must always be kept on, to keep the country running.

Thames Water has admitted wasting 600m litres of water a day. Accidents happen, but England's water companies seem unusually accident-prone. They leak about 20 per cent of the water supply, compared with 5 per cent in Germany. Worse, they routinely discharge raw sewage into rivers and onto beaches — leaving the UK bottom in Europe for bathing water quality.

Water privatisation in 1989 was seen as the route to greater efficiency and investment. But between 2002 and 2018, Scottish Water, which remains publicly owned, invested on average 35 per cent more per household than English water companies, according to Greenwich University.

In 2018, Michael Gove, environment secretary at the time, said that England's nine regional water and sewerage companies had paid out 95 per cent of their profits to shareholders between 2007 and 2016.

Clean water is a vital public service. This was shown by the tragedy of Flint, Michigan in the US, when an attempt to save money by tapping a contaminated river in 2014 led to residents being poisoned. Four government officials resigned and the water company Veolia was sued over its failure to admit that there was lead in the supply.

Last year, *Southern Water* pleaded guilty to knowingly permitting poisonous matter to enter rivers and seas for almost six years. Running its treatment plans below capacity, it had dumped raw sewage into protected seas, contaminating shellfish and acting with what the judge said was 'a wholesale disregard for the environment, for delicate ecosystems and... human health'.

The Chief Executive of *Ofwat* (the *Office of Water Regulation*), David Black, claimed that net investment had increased fourfold since privatisation. Yet Ofwat's own website says that investment has only 'roughly doubled' in that time. And *Financial Times* analysis suggests that water companies have cut investment in key infrastructure by a fifth since the 1990s. The sector has not built a single large reservoir in England for 30 years.

On leaks, the regulator is seen as weak. The industry is largely meeting the targets set — but those are less demanding than those in Germany and Denmark.

On pollution, the previous *Southern Water* penalties had made no difference to the company's behaviour. As customers, we are captives with nowhere else to go. But it takes time to accept that the cause of escalating use might be a leak, not a sudden desire by every member of a family to take baths all day. Inspecting and monitoring the network requires modern digital surveillance technologies.

Rather than issuing fines which may just get passed on to customers, one idea is to make the water companies bid for a licence to operate, against clear and stringent criteria. *Ofwat* needs to stop setting what its Chief Executive calls 'challenging but achievable targets' — a phrase which rather gives the game away. And we should perhaps let an independent campaigner chair the regulator.

One of the root problems is not getting enough accurate and timely data – to predict leaks, detect cracks and act early on problems, before they become failures.

17th November 2022

43 Cult

The Cult of Reason

'Nothing? Nothing will come of nothing. Speak again.'
– *King Lear*, I, 1

The *Cult of Reason* was France's attempt at an established state-sponsored atheistic alternative to religion, intended as a replacement for Catholicism after the French Revolution in 1789.

It was officially banned in 1802 by Napoleon Bonaparte with his Law on Cults.

Opposition to the Roman Catholic Church was one of the main causes of the French Revolution. Most of the dechristianisation of France was motivated by political concerns, but philosophical alternatives to the Church were slow in coming.

The *Cult* was a mixture of ideas and activities, and marked by chaos. Its goal was the perfection of mankind through the attainment of Truth and Liberty, and its guiding principle to this goal was the exercise of Reason.

All crosses and statues were removed from graveyards, and all cemetery gates had one inscription—'Death is an eternal sleep.'

Churches across France were transformed into modern Temples of Reason. The largest ceremony of all was at the cathedral of Notre Dame in Paris. The Christian altar was dismantled and an altar to Liberty was installed and the inscription 'To Philosophy' was carved in stone over the cathedral's doors.

Many contemporary accounts reported the Festival of Reason as a 'lurid', 'licentious' affair of scandalous 'depravities'. These accounts galvanized anti-revolutionary forces and even caused many to publicly separate themselves from the radical faction.

Maximilien Robespierre, one of the architects of the French Revolution, and the *Reign of Terror* that followed, scorned the Cult and denounced the festivals as 'ridiculous farces'.

Ancestor cults

There's a great scene in the Michael Mann film *The Last of the Mohicans*, where the British are about to be attacked by a Huron native American tribe. The Huron hesitate, and start pulling back. They realise the area is a burial ground, and the ancestors don't have to be their own relatives for them to respect this sacred earth. They do not go through with their attack.

In the novel *Christ Recrucified*, by Nikos Kazantzakis, the displaced refugee villagers look for a new area to re-start their community. They carry all their possessions across rocky terrains and mountain passes: 'the men took their tools, spades, picks, shovels; the old men lifted the icons in their arms; and then old grandfather took the lead with the sack of bones on his back.' Carrying the bones of your ancestors was a connection to the land which nourished them, with a hope that a new land will, in time, nourish them in turn too.

Professor of Religion Francesca Stavrakopoulou describes standing stones dating back to the Early Bronze Age (c. 3100 – 2000 BCE). These stones were identified with extraordinary beings. They marked the presence of deities, or deified ancestors who stood at the intersection between humans and 'otherworldly planes'. These stones were common features of temples and other ritual spaces. 'Wherever these sacred spaces were sited, their standing stones simultaneously monumentalised, memorialised and manifested the robust, grounded presence of the divine.'

These ancient ideas about divine presence played a crucial role in shaping the Bible. Something that has stood the test of time for over 2,000 years cannot be simply dismantled. Or if it is being dismantled, it is not at all clear what we are heading towards. If the universe is random, incidental and accidental, that's a hard sell to a population hungry for truth and answers. Reason is not enough. We don't derive morality from facts. It can't be done.

Man cannot move mountains. 'All we have, is the past', said novelist Anthony Burgess.

27th October 2022

44 Fall

Church and State

The Soviet Union was the first Marxist-Communist state. It rose to power following Russia's Civil War in 1921, and later became one of the world's largest and most powerful states, encompassing fifteen republics and taking control of Central and Eastern Europe following World War II.

The state not only absorbed markets, property and prices, but also limited national identity and suppressed religion. These measures were deemed essential in controlling the annexed territories. However, the Soviet Union struggled with limiting religion, specifically in Poland, a territory of strong Catholic faith. The Roman Catholic Church played a prominent economic, social, and political role in Poland, and many believe that the decline and fall of Communism is partially credited to the strength and powers of religious faith and the Church's leadership.

Religion was an outlet of social support during political and economic disruptions, a notion that the Communist regime wanted to avoid, fearing that they could no longer control its people. Dissent was a threat against its rule. Instead of people focusing on and obeying the Party, citizens turned to their faith for guidance. Although the Soviet Union did not abolish religion, it did destroy churches, create anti-religion propaganda, promote atheism, and harass clergy.

In Poland specifically, the regime launched an anti-religious campaign, persecuting monasteries and Catholic leadership in the ill-conceived hope of 'creating atheism'.

Jerzy Popiełuszko, a priest who supported the workers' union *Solidarity* through his public teachings, was one of those most prominently attacked by the Soviets. In 1984, at the age of 37, Popiełuszko was beaten to death by three officers of the Security Service of the Ministry of Internal Affairs. This effort to contain opposition in Poland and the Catholic faith only strengthened the people of Poland. At the priest's funeral, over 250,000 people attended, including Lech Wałęsa, the General Secretary of *Solidarity*, and future Polish president.

With over 93% of Poland's population in the early 1980s being practicing Catholics, church attendance reached its peak and became the centre for anti-Communist activism.

Regardless of the decreasing rates of new church developments and constant undermining in the media by the Soviet Union during the 1980s, Poland's clergy and Catholic leadership persisted, and consistently pushed their anti-Communist beliefs. In many cases, priests disobeyed the Soviet Union by giving sermons that criticised government policies. They published materials that expressed pro-democratic sentiments and re-established religious education to reach a younger audience.

To create additional instability, the Cardinal of Kraków, Karol Wojtyła, became Pope John Paul II in 1978. During his visit to his homeland in 1979, it is said that everything in Poland changed: he inspired Poles to fight peacefully for their freedom with the support of their spirituality. That same year the *Solidarity* union was formed in Gdańsk.

The Pope met with Lech Wałęsa and visited Poland multiple times despite numerous warnings from Communist authorities. At the same time, the U.S. President Ronald Reagan and U.K. Prime Minister Margaret Thatcher led the effort to undermine communism in Europe and Asia, establishing pressure on the Soviet Union.

Reaching such a large, faith-driven population, the Catholic church empowered the Polish people to protest peacefully and undermine Soviet rule to fight for their freedom. The Soviet Union's inability to control and suppress religion challenged the very nature of their political system, leading to the loss of control of its annexed territory, not only in Poland but across Eastern Europe.

The religious movements acted as a catalyst for a revolution against communism across Europe.

3rd November 2022

45 Trickle

The '*horse and sparrow*' theory of economics was first concocted in America in the 1890s. It holds that if one feeds the horses enough oats, they will eventually deposit a small sufficiency for the sparrows.

The problem is that no matter how many oats the horses eat they never leave enough for the sparrows. Since the neo-liberalism of the 1960s - 1980s, this became known as trickle-down economics.

In the book of *Deuteronomy, chapter 17*, it says that 'thou shalt set a king over thee, but he shall not multiply horses to himself, neither shall he multiply wives to himself, neither shall he greatly multiply to himself silver and gold.' The reason given for this injunction is so that 'thy heart be not lifted above thy brethren.'

One of the first laws of human decency is to take no more than your share; better still, take less than your share.

Proponents of trickle-down theory suggest that society as a whole benefits when wealth leaks down onto the poor. That it pulls up the brightest and best, who'd otherwise be undiscovered.

But are not the best among us, those who do good where they can, exercise virtue, and believe more in a job's intrinsic value than in any extra remuneration it may bring?

As for the brightest, do we mean brighter than scientists, doctors, teachers, nurses, whom our society is content to reward modestly, because it assumes that knowledge, like virtue, is its own reward? What they do, they do for the love of it.

And there we have it: *love*. Not bonuses.

Thus the argument for attracting the brightest and the best by dazzling them with baubles, fails its own test; it concedes that the brightest and the best don't have to be bribed to do what they love.

Politicians and business leaders are seeking elusive economic growth. You can boil this down to a simple question: why aren't people spending more? For one simple reason that free-marketeers rarely mention: wealthy people spend their money on personal assets – shares, land, property, houses, apartments, art. They have a higher propensity to save, not spend. These things help neither the economy, nor ordinary people. The wealth doesn't filter down.

It's spending that's needed to create income, jobs, growth and wealth. Since we have this inequality, and it is not being solved, we will have no economic recovery. It's a structural problem. We haven't fixed inequality fast enough, so we are seeing a weak economy, unaffordable housing, low wage growth, increased energy costs, inflation and falling livings standards.

Over the past twelve years, interest rates have been between zero and 1%. Businesses have taken out loans to invest in opportunities. The good investments out there to be had (start-ups, businesses growing into new markets and new technology innovations) have already been had. There just haven't been enough of them. Any excess income therefore won't be invested in businesses to trickle down from.

Since the Covid pandemic billionaires have seen a 22% increase in their wealth.

But the answer isn't to tax the rich. They go elsewhere (proven). And there aren't enough of them to make a major difference (proven). The answer is to grow the pie, not just find a better way to share the pie.

Ultimately, we need to attract investors towards regional, social and community based businesses where investments can be made locally, rooted in place and people. For us to believe in the places where we live. Ground up.

22nd December 2022

46 Idealists

'Know thyself.'
– *The Oracle at Delphi*

Karl Marx (1818-1883) is famous for three ideas: economic, political, social.

He got the last of these right, and the first two completely wrong. It's a reasonable percentage.

In economics, Marx viewed firms and industrialists as exploiters of working people. Their profits, he declared, were built on the backs of the underpaid and overworked. He downplayed the impulse to generate prosperity that comes with free enterprise. The entrepreneur takes risks, seeks investment, builds products and services that people need, employs people who then pay taxes, and empowers communities to thrive. Marx's economics was flawed, and it has proven to be unworkable in the real world. It has been tried over forty times, across world history over the past 170 years, and it has failed in every single case.

In politics, Marx took from German philosopher Friedrich Hegel (1770-1831) the idea that history is a series of reactions and counter-reactions to what came before. In technical terms, a *thesis* is adopted for a society. This is challenged over time, by an *anti-thesis*, and the collision of ideas – thesis v. anti-thesis – creates a new *synthesis*. And then we go again.

So far so good. If there were no Bush II, there would be no Obama.

Where Marx comes unstuck, is that he believed in the inevitable, inexorable direction to this historical momentum: tending towards the working class — the *proletariat* — taking control of the means of production, and creating a new order of government, known as *communism*. This has been the most devastating fallacy of the twentieth century. It's a lie that has killed seven times more people that Hitler did.

People prefer freedom to almost anything else. And we mistrust extremes. Marx misunderstood this.

Where Marx was right, however, was in his sociology. He said that, as a result of our impoverished working lives, we will feel *alienation*. Alienated from our land, our communities and our purpose. People will feel uprooted, tossed around, swimming in a stormy sea of conflicting values and uncertainty.

This one, he got spot on.

Look inside

In these confusing times of alternative facts, fake news, decline in religious observance, and uncertain values, the one thing that we can safely agree on is that *we mustn't be Nazis*.

It's the only bit of history that we know. And we don't even know it. We're still trying to come to terms with what happened in the twentieth century – to figure out the events behind the tape of the crime scene.

We must be careful with our perceived certainties. A chilling example brings this to life.

In post-war Germany, politicians had one aim: *we're not going to become like our parents*. We won't become Nazis. They think that's enough to orient their politics around. It isn't.

What happens?

The German Left begin to agree with the *Palestine Liberation Organisation*, and support their aeroplane hijackings of the 1970s. Before you know it, one of the German left-wing politicians, Hans-Joachim Klein, is on the plane, as it's on the tarmac during one hijacking, and he's separating out the Jews and the non-Jews.

Eh? What? We've done it again! The one thing we were meant NOT to become, was the people standing on the ramps, saying 'You go right. You go left'. And we did it. We went all the way round!

Your enemies don't always come with jackboots and swastikas.

They live inside you.

47 Singapore

Singapore-on-Thames: An elite scam, or a way forward?

Singapore is a successful city state. High wealth, low crime, high educational attainment (worldwide Top Five for Maths), legitimate institutions and stable government. Its government ministers are paid $1m per annum.

There is a strand of modern, liberal, conservative economic thinking that believes that this model could be applied to the United Kingdom. This was a driver that fuelled Liz Truss's short-lived, ultimately untried but widely mistrusted autumnal 'project', in September and October of 2022.

Could this work in the UK? What are the pros and cons of 'Singapore-on-Thames'?

Pros:

1. Effective Governance: efficient, quick decision-making. The UK could experience increased productivity and faster policy implementation.
2. Economic Growth: a thriving economy with emphasis on trade and investment.
3. Cleanliness and Safety: Singapore is known for its clean environment and low crime.

Cons:

1. Lack of Democratic Freedoms: Singapore has a reputation for being authoritarian, with limited freedom of expression and strict censorship laws.
2. High Cost of Living: expensive housing and transportation.
3. Cultural Differences: The UK and Singapore have different cultural backgrounds and values. The Singapore model may not work well in a multicultural, diverse society like the UK. Having said that, 40% of Singapore's population is immigrant (compared to the UK's 17%).

Classical City States

It is worth looking at the history of city states, most prominent among which are the ancient Greek city-states – Athens, Sparta, Corinth, Thebes, and Syracuse, among others. They were successful through their strategic location, economic and cultural advancements, and military prowess.

Geographically, the city-states controlled trade routes, such as the Black Sea and the Mediterranean. They held valuable resources and accumulated wealth through trade.

The Greeks were also known for their cultural and intellectual achievements, in philosophy, literature, and architecture. Their achievements gave them a unique identity and helped establish ties with other civilisations.

The Greeks were skilled warriors and developed sophisticated military technologies. This protected their territories and expanded their influence through conquest.

However, the Greek city-states fell into decline through constant internal conflicts and instability. The city-states were constantly at odds with one another, which made it hard to form alliances, and defend against external threats.

Another factor was their inability to adapt to changing geopolitical circumstances. The rise of the powerful Roman Empire overshadowed the Greek city-states, and rendered them militarily insignificant.

Finally, the Greek city-states were weakened by a series of wars, including the Peloponnesian War, which depleted resources and left them vulnerable to invasion. Ultimately, Greek city-states were absorbed into larger empires and lost their independence.

National cultures

Another lens through which to examine the compatibility and exportability of regimes to different nationalities, is the work of social psychologist Geert Hofstede. He identified different forms of national culture and placed countries, and corporations looking to expand there, on a sliding scale of extremes.

Individual and collectivism: This considers whether individuals believe they should look after themselves rather than be team players. The UK and the USA tend towards the *individual*, contrasting with Singapore, which is more *collective*.

Power distance index (PDI): Does a society accept power being distributed? Countries where PDI is low will have decentralised organisations, whereas countries with a high PDI have centralised, hierarchical structures. UK has devolved assemblies and accepts decentralisation across its

70m population. Singapore has a very centralised system for its 6m people.

Masculinity: This refers to dominant values in the organisation. Are these 'masculine' (assertiveness, money) or 'feminine' (concern for others, quality of relationships)? No comment.

Long-term orientation: This refers to how long-term the thinking is – in planning and investment horizons. Singapore has a twenty year perspective. The UK considers how things will play on social media in the next hour, and what will lead on the day's news bulletins.

Overall, London as a city state seems antithetical to *Levelling Up* – the idea of greater economic alignment across the nation. It sounds elitist, and amplifies the southern, rarefied lifestyles.

11th May 2023

48 Defeat

Honour (*meiyo*) | Tradition (*dentou*) | Values (*kachikan*)

In 1944, after many years of war, the tide was turning against Japan.

The territories they had won throughout the Pacific were now toppling like dominoes to U.S. forces.

Defeat seemed inevitable.

In December, 1944, Second Lieutenant Hiroo Onoda of the Japanese Imperial Army was deployed to the small island of Lubang in the Philippines. His orders were to slow down the United States' progress, and to never surrender.

In February 1945, the Americans arrived on Lubang and took the island. Most of the Japanese soldiers surrendered, but Onoda hid in the jungle.

He began a guerrilla campaign against the U.S. forces and the local population. That August, the United States dropped atomic bombs on Hiroshima and Nagasaki. Japan surrendered, and the war came to its dramatic conclusion.

Not the end

However, thousands of Japanese soldiers were still scattered among the Pacific isles. Many, like Onoda, were hiding in the jungle, unaware that the war was over.

The U.S. military and the Japanese government dropped thousands of leaflets throughout the Pacific region, announcing that the war was over and it was time for everyone to go home. Onoda decided that they were fake, an American trap. He stayed hidden.

In 1952, letters and pictures from his family were airdropped, along with a personal note from the Emperor himself. Onoda refused to listen.

In 1972, both the Japanese and Philippine governments sent search parties to look for the enigmatic lieutenant. They found nothing.

The story of Lieutenant Onoda became an urban legend in Japan – was he real?

Around this time, a young man named Norio Suzuki first heard of Onoda. Suzuki believed that he would be the one to find Onoda.

Unarmed and untrained in warfare, Suzuki travelled to Lubang and wandered around the jungle alone. His strategy: scream Onoda's name loudly and tell him the Emperor was worried about him.

He found Onoda in four days.

Suzuki stayed with Onoda in the jungle for some time. Onoda welcomed the companionship, and wanted to learn about the world. They became friends.

Meaning

We choose to dedicate time to seemingly useless causes. It's hard to imagine how Onoda could have been happy on that island living off insects and sleeping rough.

Onoda said he regretted nothing – it had been an honour to devote his life in service. He chose how he wished to suffer – loyalty to empire. Because it meant something, he could endure it, even enjoy it.

If our problems are inevitable and unavoidable, the question we should ask is not 'How do I stop suffering?' but 'For what purpose am I suffering?'

Fame

Second Lieutenant Hiroo Onoda returned to Japan in 1974 as a celebrity.

What he found horrified him: a consumerist, superficial culture that had lost the tradition of honour and sacrifice upon which his generation was raised.

Onoda used his fame to promote the values of the Old Japan. But he was seen as a showpiece from a time-capsule for everyone to marvel at – a museum relic.

Irony of ironies, Onoda became more depressed than he'd ever been in the jungle. There, his life stood for something. It made his suffering endurable.

Back in Japan, in what he considered to be a vacuous nation full of hippies and loose women in Western clothing, he confronted an unavoidable truth: his fighting meant nothing.

The Japan he had fought for no longer existed. This realisation pierced him in a way that no bullet ever had.

In 1980, Onoda moved to Brazil, where he remained until he died, aged 91.

1st June 2023

XII – Greeks

ΝΙΨΟΝΑΝΟΜΗΜΑΤΑΜΗΜΟΝΑΝΟΨΙΝ

Νίψον ανομήματα μη μόναν όψιν

'Wash away your sins, not only your face.'

> – *The longest known palindrome in literature (Guinness Book of Records), and inscribed on the courtyard fountains of many Greek Orthodox churches*

49 Honey

Without bees, life wouldn't exist on our planet.

While prosperous countries have struggled to keep their honeybees alive, Greece continues to produce the world's finest honey. Few countries love honey and revere beekeepers more than Greece, and no country has a deeper history in this craft.

Beekeeping came to Greece as early as 1500 BCE from the Hittites, an ancient group of Indo-Europeans who moved into Asia Minor to form Anatolia. Their laws declared the punishment for theft of a hive (5 shekels of silver, about the same as for stealing a sheep). In Athens, archaeologists have excavated hives made from pottery dating to 400 BCE, which often were reused as coffins for children.

Seventy percent of the world's agriculture depends on bees

Today, the average Greek consumes approximately 3.6 pounds of honey a year, the largest amount per capita in the European Union and more than double the U.S consumption.

Greece has the greatest density of bee colonies in Europe, with 11.4 colonies per square kilometre. At the 2019 London Honey Awards, judges bestowed prizes on 17 Greek honey producers, crowning them with three of five possible platinum awards.

While bee colonies around the world have been dying at an alacritous rate, dragging down worldwide honey production, Greece's honey industry has remained stable, producing honey that is widely praised, and among the most potent in the world, containing antibacterial and antioxidant properties.

With Greek unemployment dangerously high at around 18 percent, beekeeping is still flourishing — an economic refuge for some, and a growing cottage industry.

In July 2019, the *Earthwatch Institute* declared the honeybee 'the most important living being on earth.' The reason is that 70 percent of the world's agriculture depends on bees. Yet we've managed to let this insect's population decline so dramatically that bees are now considered an endangered species.

Nearly a quarter of Greece's 5,700 plant species are unique to the country. And Greece's dry summer heat and minimal rainfall give its plants and herbs, such as thyme, oregano, and sage, an unusually intense potency.

Beekeepers use genetic selection to choose queens that will build strong colonies. To clear the way for a new queen, they need to overturn the will of the worker bees. They eliminate the hive's developing bee larvae, which the worker bees feed with protein-rich royal jelly to create their own queen.

A queen's powerful pheromones stop other worker bees from laying eggs, and this then unifies the hive around her. Once she becomes queen, her job is to lay eggs—as many as 1,500 a day. A queen can lay eggs for as long as 6 years, outliving all other members of the colony.

In June of 2019, the *Bee Informed Partnership*, a U.S.-based research collaborative, released its annual survey of nearly 5,000 American beekeepers and reported the loss of

40 percent of colonies over the previous year. The European Commission reported losses in some member countries of 50 percent or more.

Rising commodity prices have encouraged farmers to plant every inch of their fields in corn or soybeans. Those fields are now planted with seeds engineered to be resistant to the fungicides, herbicides, and pesticides that farmers increasingly use.

Scientists agree that high bee death rates stem from a complex mix of pesticide exposure, mite infestation, habitat loss, and climate change, but they disagree about the relative importance of each factor.

In 1993, the U.S. had about 2.9 million bee colonies that produced some 231 million pounds of honey. By 2017, honey output dropped 36 percent to 148 million pounds. One result: more than two-thirds of the honey consumed in the U.S. is now imported.

10th November 2022

50 Secret

Clandestine school

'My language, my soul.'
– *Odysseas Elytis*

How did the Greek language miraculously survive almost four hundred years under the yoke of Turkish-Ottoman rule (1453 – 1821)?

Greek has a rich and complex history that has seen it survive multiple conquests and occupations throughout the centuries. During the Ottoman Empire's domination of Greece from the 15th century to the 19th century, the Greek language faced cultural suppression and forced assimilation.

Despite these challenges, the language has survived. A primary reason is that the Greek Orthodox Church played a critical role in preserving the language and the culture of Greece. The church served as a bastion of Greek identity and language, and it continued to educate and inform the Greek people about their cultural heritage.

Additionally, the Greek language was kept alive through the efforts of Greek scholars and writers who preserved their culture. They produced literature, poetry, and historical works in Greek, which kept the language thriving.

The Nobel laureate Isaac Bashevis Singer wrote in Yiddish, which many believed to be a dead language. He said he did so for two reasons. First, he said that he liked ghosts, and this befits a so-called dead language. And second, he believed in resurrection. 'One day', he said, 'when the Messiah comes, all these Jews will be walking around, asking, '*Are there any good new Yiddish stories to read*?' '

The Greek War of Independence, 1821, marked a turning point in the history of the Greek language. The struggle for independence helped to revive Greek nationalism, and created the modern Greek state, which provided fertile ground to develop modern Greek.

In Greek history, a *krifó scholió* ('secret school') was an underground school for teaching the language and Christian doctrine, provided by the Orthodox Church.

Historians accept that these secret schools existed during periods of intense Islamisation. School textbooks in Greece treated the *krifó scholió* as factual until the late 20th century, when it was finally removed, despite some political controversy, as a 'national memory which had been, to some extent, fictitious'.

The Ottoman authorities prohibited education in the languages of its non-Muslim subjects, obliging Greeks to organise small, secret schools in monasteries and churches. Some of them were kept open through bribing influential Turks. The official school of Smyrna was persecuted because it taught mathematics and philosophy.

The narrative of secret schools became popular after the 1821 Revolution. It became more entrenched in the collective memory of Greeks through a painting by Nikolaos Gyzis called '*Greek school in the time of slavery*' (1886). It depicts a romanticised school scene. A distinguished looking priest reads by candlelight with a group of youths.

Within the Ottoman system, the Ecumenical Patriarchate of Constantinople was responsible for civil administration for the Christian population, and had a high degree of autonomy in running its own affairs. Hence the church was free to run schools wherever it desired.

Ottoman administration did not try to forbid Greek or Christian schools, but instead patriotic consciousness was spread through secret lessons given in secret places by teachers promoting national liberation.

In 2019, I visited Meteora in northern Greece. The region has six monasteries perched, astoundingly, upon huge rock pillars. Inside one of the monasteries, I saw an original letter, centuries old, from the local Sultan ruler (Agha), instructing the surrounding villages and towns to leave the monastery in peace. Nobody was to disrupt or attack or harm any of its surrounding fields, orchards and lands. The inhabitants must be allowed to continue their peaceful, monastic endeavours, and their agriculture, their beekeeping and grape cultivation, among other pursuits.

An enlightened directive, hinting at tolerance, collaboration, understanding and leniency.

XIII – Language

'He's a man with a fork in a world of soup.'

– Noel Gallagher on brother Liam

A Greek man ...

The Greek Orthodox priest of the village is getting ready to leave his house to go to his church to conduct the Sunday service. It's raining pretty hard. But he can't find his umbrella. He looks everywhere, but it's nowhere to be found. Annoyed, he is convinced that someone has stolen it, and vows there and then to catch the thief.

He arrives at church, soaking wet. He calls over to George, the altar helper.

He says, 'George, listen, someone has stolen my umbrella, and you're going to help me find the thief.'

'Of course, Father,' says George, 'what can I do to help?'

The priest outlines his plan. 'Today, I'll be talking about the *Ten Commandments*. And when I get to the commandment that says '*Thou shalt not steal*', I'm going to stop. And then, George, in that silence, I want you to take a good look around our congregation. Whoever is shifting in his seat, or whoever turns red, or if anyone looks agitated and uncomfortable – that's our thief!'

'Right you are, Father,' says George.

The service starts and eventually it's time for the sermon. The priest begins on the commandments, and goes through them. He says, 'Thou shalt not murder... Thou shalt not commit adultery ... thou shalt not steal ... thou shalt not bear false witness against thy neighbour ... ', but he just continues, going through each one, without stopping, and finishes his sermon.

The church service is over. George goes up to the priest. 'But Father, you didn't stop at *Thou shalt not steal*. I couldn't see ... I didn't have time to check on who the thief might be.'

51 Jokes

'The film director Luis Buñuel used to say: 'I would give my life for a man who is looking for the truth. But I would gladly kill a man who thinks he has found the truth.' (This is what we used to call a joke, before killing people for their ideas returned to the agenda.)'
– *Sir Salman Rushdie (1990)*

Mothers: I

My mum bought me two ties for Christmas.
I wore one of them on New Year's Eve.
She said, 'Aha! So you didn't like the other one, then.'

Mothers: II

Christ is talking to a crowd. There is a commotion and some people are about to stone Mary Magdalene. He intervenes and says his piece.

Then he says, 'Whoever is without sin among you, let them cast the first stone.'

A heavy rock hits Jesus on the head. He looks up, and shouts, 'Mum! I told you to stay at home.'

The priest replies, 'Ah, it's OK, George. Don't worry about it. As soon as I said, *Thou shalt not commit adultery …* I remembered where I left my umbrella.'

And a Jew …

Sarah is caught stealing peaches.

She is on trial, in front of the Rabbi.

'How many peaches did you steal, Sarah?, asks the Rabbi.

'Rabbi, I stole five peaches,' replies Sarah.

'Five peaches, you stole. So for five peaches, Sarah, you will get five nights in prison,' declared the Rabbi.

'Rabbi,' gasps Sarah, 'But my family, my kids. Wow, five nights away I have to be?'

'That's the law, sorry, Sarah. Five peaches, five nights,' says the Rabbi.

Sarah is upset as she takes all this in. There's a silence.

Suddenly, Sarah's husband, Nathan, who's been sitting quietly up until then, calls out.

'And, as it happens, Rabbi. If I may. She also stole a can of peas.'

22nd September 2022

52 Italiano

Se non hai mai pianto, I tuoi occhi non possono essere belli
'If you haven't cried, your eyes can't be beautiful.'
– *Sophia Loren*

The Italian Prime Minister Giorgia Meloni is resisting the invasion of the English language, as it encroaches on everyday Italian life.

The claim is that the 'obsessive' use of English risks causing the 'gradual disappearance' of the Italian language. The bill aims to prohibit all foreign words, but claims that English is a particular danger, with the adoption over years of words and phrases such as 'management', 'car sharing' and 'sexy shop' to describe a retailer of lacy underwear.

Italy has been here before. Among the words banned in the 1930s were 'cocktail', which became 'bevanda arlecchina' or 'Harlequin drink' because it could be multicoloured. Louis Armstrong's name was Italianised to *Luigi Braccioforte*.

This current incarnation is part of a new prohibition trend, that Italy seems to be leading the world in. It marks another step in the ringfencing of Italian culture by Meloni's right-wing government, which has just become the first country is the world to officially ban the AI application *ChatGPT*. They have also banned synthetic meat made in laboratories last month to 'protect traditional Italian cuisine.'

La lingua Inglese

A government bill, proposed by Meloni's party, *Brothers of Italy*, warns that 9,000 English words have crept into Italian use and are now recorded in the dictionary.

Italian companies using English words in their work could face fines of up to €100,000.

In 2015, 70,000 Italians signed a petition to halt the invasion of English words after the navy used the slogan '*Be Cool and Join the Navy*'.

Claudio Marazzini, the head of Italy's linguistic academy, convinced Italy to use the expression 'lavoro agile' instead of 'smart working'.

Critics recalled that Meloni's party had descended from the *MSI* party, a post-war fascist movement, and compared the bill to the ban on foreign words imposed by the fascist dictator Benito Mussolini.

Valeria Della Valle, a linguist, suggested that Meloni's government was suffering from the serious affliction called nostalgia, and said: 'Fines for the use of foreign words have a history I would rather not relive.'

Carne e 'omicidio

In a similar vein, the ominous charge of 'decadence' was used as the government proposes to ban plant based meat. The law outlawing the use of laboratory-produced food and animal feed aims to safeguard the country's agriculture and its proud food heritage.

'Laboratory products in our opinion do not guarantee quality, well-being and the protection of our culture, or our tradition,' said Minister Francesco Lollobrigida.

Meloni's nationalist administration has pledged to shield Italy's food from technological innovations seen as harmful, and renamed the agriculture ministry the 'Ministry for Agriculture and Food Sovereignty'.

Activists for the agriculture lobby have praised the move against 'synthetic food', saying a ban is needed to safeguard home production 'from the attacks of multinational companies'. The bill stipulates that factories where violations occur can be shut down and producers may lose their right to receive public funding.

The initiative angered organisations supporting the development of 'cell-based' agricultural products across Europe, as well as animal rights groups.

'The passing of such a law would shut down the economic potential of this nascent field in Italy, holding back scientific progress and climate mitigation efforts,' said Alice Ravenscroft, head of policy at the *Good Food Institute Europe*.

Food companies' network *Cellular Agriculture Europe* said that Italy was limiting options for consumers who are concerned about animal welfare, and the environmental impact of their food choices.

20th April 2023

53 Speech

Cadence and rhythm: And the words that work

Dr. Martin Luther King's '*I Have a Dream*' speech was crafted in a rich, imaginative language that helped people to see the potential that could be ahead of them.

The speech is only sixteen minutes long, and follows a compelling three pillar arc: What is. What could be. The new bliss.

Most people in America in 1963 had not heard a Southern Baptist preacher before. It was the first time that such a speech was broadcast nationally. The Southern Baptist oral tradition is infused with rhythm and cadence and long dramatic pauses.

A number of devices make the speech one of the most heard ever. These are: repetition, metaphor, familiarity, and political reference.

1. Repetition. This is a rhetorical style that was made especially strong by King, often using the power of threes. It drives the point home, and the audience gets caught up in the rhythm.

'***Now is the time***, *to rise from the dark and desolate valley of segregation to the sunlit path of racial justice.*

***Now is the time**, to lift our nation from the quicksands of racial injustice to the solid rock of brotherhood.*

***Now is the time**, to make justice a reality.'*

2. Metaphors and visual words. Strong emphasis on painting vivid scenes, and helping his audience to *see* what he's saying.

'We have come to cash this cheque, that promises us the riches of freedom, and the security of justice.'

3. Familiar songs, scripture and literature. These are especially dear to the African-American community. This involves using biblical quotations, popular folk songs, slave spirituals and Gospel music.

Towards the end of the speech, King quotes from the Old Testament book of Isaiah, urging his audience to demand their rights: *'An exile in our own land'*, refers to Moses leading his people to freedom.

There's even some Shakespeare in there, too: *'This sweltering summer of legitimate discontent.'*

And true to his mentor, we can detect some Gandhi as well. In a rebuke to the violent tactics of Malcolm X, King implores his audience, again using repetition:-

*'**We must** forever conduct our campaign on the high plain of dignity and discipline.*

***We must** not allow our creative protests to degenerate into physical violence.*

***We must** rise to the majestic heights of meeting physical force with soul force.'*

'*Soul-force*' was a term coined by Gandhi – *Satyagraha*. It fuelled the struggle of civil disobedience in the campaign for a free India.

This was King's 'marvellous new militancy'. A non-violent one. And in the phrase '*We cannot walk alone*', he reaches out to the white community.

4. Political references. Here, historical documents are mentioned, such as the *Declaration of Independence*, and the *Emancipation Proclamation,* both of which promised freedom.

It is when King combines all these devices: repetition, metaphor, songs, references: that his speech catches fire.

He says:-

'***One hundred years later***, *we are still not free.*

One hundred years later, *we are still manacled by the chains of discrimination.*

One hundred years later, *we live on a lonely island of poverty, in the midst of a vast ocean of prosperity.*'

The speech was palpable and urgent. It wasn't a doctoral thesis. It used a demotic and powerful language.

King said he had a *dream*. He didn't say, *I have a plan*. Or a blueprint, or a roadmap, or a strategy. That would have been too technocratic, and would have turned his audience off.

He took risks to get this message out. His house was bombed, he was stabbed, he was shot. Ultimately, he lost his life.

The lesson is to reach into an audience and light a spark that resonates with them. Audience-centric, client-centric, student-centric.

'*What's in it for me?*' is the only question that most people tend to ask.

4th May 2023

54 Manc

Is the Manc accent disappearing?

'But this is Manchester. We do things differently here.'
– *Tony Wilson*

A major feature of the 'Manc' accent is disappearing – but not in North Manchester. New linguistics research at *The University of Manchester* found that the traditional 'Manc' accent is still going strong in northern parts of the city, but is vanishing elsewhere.

Dr Maciej Baranowski looked for any linguistic evidence for the popular view that the north Manchester accent sounds different from the one spoken in south Manchester. He talked to people from areas within the M60 motorway, as well as those to the south, such as Wythenshawe and Stockport.

He found that the so-called 'north-force distinction' – where words like *four* and *wore* have a different vowel sound to *for* and *war* – is disappearing in the south and centre of the city. It has completely disappeared from the speech of middle-class Mancunians, so for them, the words in these pairs sound identical - as for most speakers of English today.

The Manchester accent is a reflex of Middle English, with a lengthened vowel before the /r/ in *horse, fork, for, morning*, so these words sound like: *hoarse, four-k, four, mourning*.

Neighbourhood factor

Although the idea that different parts of a city sound different is popular among non-linguists, there is no evidence for this. Wherever differences between neighbourhoods have been discovered, they are usually social class distinctions. If particular parts of a city are inhabited by certain socioeconomic groups, then those neighbourhoods sound different from other parts of the city. Speakers with the same socioeconomic backgrounds will have the same sound system regardless of their geographic provenance.

'*Brooklynese*', for example, which is supposedly the accent of the borough of Brooklyn in New York City, actually turns out to be the accent of working-class New Yorkers, whether they grew up in Brooklyn, Queens, or the Bronx. Researchers Becker and Newlin-Lukowicz confirmed this lack of geographic differentiation, showing that New Yorkers cannot correctly identify which borough speakers come from on the basis of audio samples.

North Manchester is largely working-class, with a closer-knit, less mobile community, in comparison with south Manchester. This preserves older dialects. South Manchester has an influx of middle-class speakers from outside the city. So middle-class Mancunians, who tend to live in central / south Manchester, use accents that are closer to the south of England, as in the fronting of *goat* – '*go-oot*' – instead of the Mancunian '*gort*'.

Additionally, having continued contact with relatives, a working-class child growing up in north Manchester is much less likely to be exposed to *merged* speakers, and is more likely to preserve their parents' and grandparents' speech.

The spellings of these words give a clue about how different they once sounded, but 'dialect levelling' means that British English is more uniform than it was. Some long-standing accents are disappearing – the traditional working-class *Cockney* accent is said to be weakening, but *Multicultural London English* is becoming more widespread.

Maciej says the Manc accent will be around for some time, especially in nearby towns to the north, like Rochdale, Bolton and Oldham.

Demographic changes over recent years have seen employers including *Google*, *Amazon*, *Microsoft* and the *BBC* relocating jobs to Manchester, and a population boom with tens of thousands of highly-educated workers arriving in the city, especially from overseas. Maciej did not set out to assess whether this has had a linguistic effect on the city, but it's likely to accelerate changes already happening to the accent.

XIV – Sport

'You miss 100 percent of the shots you don't take.'

– Wayne Gretzky

55 Klopp

Klopp-tastic: Affectionate, intimate, safe, loving leadership

'Prepare Relentlessly'
– *Chapter 3, 'Leadership', Rudy Giuliani*

When Liverpool beat Chelsea in the FA Cup Final on 14th May 2022, the five minutes after the final whistle made all the difference.

With the score at 0-0 after extra time, the match went to penalties. A penalty shootout is a psychological game, starting with how the manager communicates with his players. Liverpool manager Jürgen Klopp and Chelsea manager Thomas Tuchel spent those five minutes very differently.

60 seconds after the final whistle: Klopp has already made his selection of who will take the penalties. He approaches each penalty taker to tell / ask him which number shot to take. He does this one-on-one and often cements his ask with his trademark hug. The asking process is intimate, safe and loving.

At 1 minute and 30 seconds: Klopp is done with his rounds, the team is gathered in a huddle, and he gives a short but passionate speech.

At 1 minute and 45 seconds: he finishes and the team breaks up the huddle.

At 1 minute and 50 seconds: Tuchel is meanwhile still revising his notes, and eventually making his way to the huddle.

Tuchel spent the first 1 – 2 minutes seemingly revising his selection, and (probably) from the corner of his eye he sees that Liverpool have already finished their huddle before Chelsea have even started it. He then moves into the middle of the circle before he is finished with the plan.

Entering the circle of players before you've completed the selection is what happened to Gareth Southgate in the 2021 Euros final – you're late, not ready, become reactive, and what could have been a smooth final reminder to the team becomes erratic, rushed and stressed.

In the huddle, Tuchel then asks his players about the shots, publicly, in front of the whole team. There's plenty of group pressure when it's done this way – and the chance of an honest response from the players inevitably drops. It creates further stress that carries on into the shootout itself.

While Tuchel is still in the process of selecting and asking his players, Klopp has finished all his administrative duties and spends his time spreading warmth, love and good energy. Even taking a moment to have a laugh with defender Virgil van Dijk.

Because Liverpool finished their huddle early, they step into the middle circle first, and get to pick position. They choose the side closest to their bench, which enables the staff to give further instructions during the shootout. It also maintains the closeness to the warmth of the manager.

Jürgen Klopp's deliberate and substantial attention to *team mentality* is not just born, it's made, and it's cultivated. Proactive preparation, composed execution, and empathetic, affectionate communication – all these things give the best possible foundation for a performance under extreme pressure.

Liverpool were psychologically 1-0 up before a single penalty was taken.

Even though Liverpool's Sadio Mané missed his penalty, he's soon laughing in the centre circle with his fellow players. The cup wasn't yet won, but they were so relaxed. It reminded me of the movie *The Right Stuff*, about the first astronauts. For a moment, Mission Control loses contact with Gordo Cooper (played by Dennis Quaid), who's in position on the launchpad. Then they hear snoring. He is so relaxed that he falls asleep just before launch.

Let's not forget the goalkeeper. After every penalty he faced, Liverpool's Alisson Becker retrieved the ball and made sure he handed it to the next Liverpool player. Whereas Edouard Mendy (his opposite number) and the Chelsea players seemed like strangers.

26th May 2023

56 Philosophy

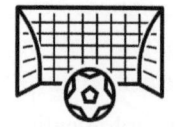

'All that I know most surely about morality and obligations, I owe to football.'

– *Albert Camus*

Mutual respect, discipline, understanding and a sense of team spirit are as important in football, as they are in our communities.

A football academy – *Academie des Gardiens De But* – based in the pretty spa town of Luchon, in south-west France, is re-inventing the fusion of sport and community.

Drawing inspiration from two illustrious predecessors – World Cup-winning goalkeeper Fabien Barthez, and the author Albert Camus – the unique institution aims to instil the values of citizenship in 11-16-year-olds from around the world and from all walks of life.

Technical Director Jacques Julia says, 'Every time a child saves a ball it's similar to difficult situations they will face in life. Every time they go into a tackle, they need courage and commitment.'

Julia knows the importance of instilling the values of fair play and discipline within sport to young people who have lost their way in life. He has worked in the most deprived areas of France, known as the *banlieue* (suburbs), where disaffected youths became embroiled in crime, fought running battles with police and set property and cars alight, during rioting around Paris and other cities.

One of those behind the project is Barthez, the former *Manchester United* and France goalkeeper, who, despite a long career at the top, never lost sight of where he came from.

'We're trying to get away from the idea of producing champions - we're interested in promoting good morals among young adults,' he says. 'It's important for our pupils to learn to become men. I want to give back to football what it has given to me.' As well as the football and life-skills coaching, the students will also receive a conventional education, in line with France's school curriculum.

'We've come here to progress in school as much as in football - gaining and developing good values is important to us,' says Jeremie de Aldiah, 15.

Resilience

Local businesses, the French Football Association, and Nike are all supporting the academy. English Premier League clubs are watching the academy's progress closely.

'Whilst French keepers Fabien Barthez and Elie Baup were the inspiration for the academy, there are parallels with Camus' writing', says Julia, a former *Toulouse FC* coach.

An influential author and thinker, Camus was a semi-professional goalkeeper for the national title-winning *Racing Universitaire Algerois* in his native Algeria before turning to his literary pursuits.

In 1942 he wrote *L'Etranger* (*The Outsider*), his most influential book, which expresses through its protagonist, Meursault, Camus' view that life has no rational or perceptible meaning. This central theme saw Camus continually state his belief that the universal struggle to attach structure and meaning to our lives is ultimately futile and, in his words, absurd.

The Rebel

The notion of 'the absurd' Camus put forward in *L'Etranger* and in his essay, *The Myth of Sisyphus*, led indirectly to the revival of 'absurdism' in modern theatre and philosophy.

Like all the best cult heroes, Camus was a committed anti-authoritarian. During the Nazi occupation of France he was active in the French resistance and, in his work *L'Homme Révolté*, he put forward a savage critique of the Soviet state and of revolutionary politics.

We can consider football as a metaphor for our lives: there are similarities between football (rules, roles) and our everyday life of work, friends, and family. It's a school of life – being in a group, learning to make sacrifices, and to be responsible, altruistic (passing the ball) and humble. To be loyal, and to be an example to our companions.

57 Onanistic

Onanistic elites: And loving football

In 2014, Dutch journalist Wim Kayzer interviewed 26 eminent people for the TV series '*Of beauty and comfort*'. He asked scientists, writers, philosophers, artists and musicians: 'What makes this life worth living?'

Twenty of them then gathered in Amsterdam for a discussion. It became a three hour film. An evening with Simon Schama, Richard Rorty, Sir Roger Scruton, Germaine Greer, George Steiner, Martha Nussbaum, Jane Goodall, Wole Soyinka, and some other people that I haven't heard of: Dubravka Ugresic, John Coetzee, Leon Lederman, Tatjana Tolstaja, Freeman Dyson, Elizabeth Loftus, Gary Lynch, Catherine Bott, Rutger Kopland, Rudi Fuchs, György Konrád, and Karel Appel.

A sparkling highlight was the following exchange on football.

Germaine Greer: Football is an enormous global phenomenon. It commands vast amounts of money. Every single person watching it is an expert; can discuss it for hours. Bertolt Brecht said that what he wanted from a theatre audience was the same intelligent detachment and passion as in a sports crowd. It is the legitimate cultural expression in

Britain. It finances itself; it doesn't need to plunder anybody; it doesn't need to lie and bullshit and grandstand. We have totally mediocre people running the arts establishment in England, and geniuses running football. And the music is great.

It's important not to be snobbish about football. That culture is hostile to us because the arts establishment has withdrawn unto itself, patted itself on the back, invited itself to cocktail parties. We became an onanistic elite, and football is our punishment.

George Steiner: Let's have a moment of modesty about our small brains. The best historical estimate is there were 10 people at Golgotha. We can say there were 1,100 at the premiere of *Hamlet*. There were 1,400 at Beethoven's first *Missa Solemnis*. Watching the World Cup Final, were 2.5 billion people. We can't take in what that means.

When Karl Marx says quantity leaps into absolute quality, he's right. When Maradona is running towards the goal, the heart rates of two and a half billion people are racing.

The comic side, was that the *English Water Board* issued a polite statement: '*Try to avoid all going to the toilet at the same moment at half time – we can't handle it!*' No Shakespeare, no Beethoven has had the loo system suspended for human emotion. How do we handle such a planetary emotion?

Sir Roger Scruton: One important distinction surely, George, is that from those ten people at Golgotha, an emotion has been passed on down the centuries, increasing, so that across time, diachronically, the weight of emotion is enormous, and is also carrying on. Whereas those 2.5 billion ephemeral heart-beats have gone, forever. It means nothing. And after those 1,400 at the *Missa Solemnis,* over the next 170 years, there have been another billion more emotional vibrations. It goes on vibrating. You can return to that perfect object that encapsulates within itself the meaning of that experience.

Germaine Greer: There *is* something transcendent about football. I have a friend who is a cell biologist. He works at the cutting edge of the proteins involved in Alzheimer's and Parkinson's. I asked him, 'How did you feel when *Cambridge United* were promoted?', and he said, 'I was walking on air.' Whereas the discovery of a new protein did *not* make him walk on air.

George Steiner: Every child in Newcastle knows the quotation, 'Football is not a matter of life and death. It's much more important than that.'

Well, you're absolutely right, dearly departed and beloved George, they do know it in Newcastle, as well as in Liverpool, and everywhere else.

25th May 2023

58 Physics

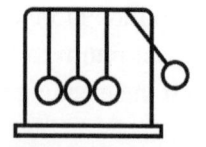

On June 3, 1997, Roberto Carlos stunned the world with one of the most spectacular free kicks in football history.

The left-back scored an outrageous long-range dead-ball shot for Brazil in a 1-1 draw against France in the 1997 *Tournoi de France* (a warm-up tournament before the following year's World Cup in France).

The strike left goalkeeper Fabien Barthez perplexed, as the ball apparently was heading wide of the goal and into the crowd. However, it swerved back, glanced the inside edge of the post, and hit the back of the net.

'I don't know how I did that,' he told ESPN Brazil. 'It required a lot of training and hard work throughout my career, which paid off. A special moment.'

When he scored the goal, the left-back was in his second season at *Real Madrid*. In Madrid, he would win titles, and become an idol. He is an ambassador for the club. He became Brazil's starting left-back in the 1998, 2002 and 2006 World Cups, winning it in South Korea/Japan (2002), having been a runner-up in France four years earlier.

'I never tried to kick like that again, because I know I would never have scored,' he says. 'Someday someone will score a similar goal.'

The impossible kick?

The goal defied physics and still impresses scientists today. Physicists around the world studied and analysed the aerodynamics of the ball's curve that day in Lyon.

One of the most famous studies was conducted by four French scientists – Guillaume Dupeux, Anne Le Goff, David Quere and Christophe Clanet – and published in the *New Journal of Physics* in September 2010. The physicists conducted several experiments which resulted in an equation that explains the ball's trajectory and the forces that were in action at that precise moment.

'In this case, $\mathcal{L}$ is twice as small as L. The ball trajectory can deviate significantly from a circle, provided that the shot is long enough. Then the trajectory becomes surprising and unpredictable for a goalkeeper,' they wrote.

'This is the way we interpret the famous goal by Roberto Carlos. This free kick was shot from a distance of approximately 35 metres, that is, comparable to the distance for which we expect this kind of unexpected trajectory. Provided that the shot is powerful enough, another characteristic of Roberto Carlos' abilities, the ball trajectory brutally bends towards the net, at a velocity still large enough to surprise the keeper.'

Dupeux, Le Goff, Quere and Clanet conclude that if the correct calculations were made, and the distances and forces were repeated, the famous goal could be replicated by another player. This is impossible in the opinion of one of Brazil's most important physicists. He describes Roberto Carlos' masterpiece as a 'football miracle'.

'Although physics explain perfectly the ball's trajectory, the conditions in that moment, such as the power of the kick, the point of impact of Roberto Carlos' foot on the ball, and the distance to the goal, were so rare that we can call that a miracle,' says Professor Luis Fernando Fontanari of *Sao Carlos Physics Institute*, a branch of the *University of Sao Paulo*.

Fontanari is editor of scientific journals '*Physics of Life Reviews*' and '*Theory in Biosciences*'. He adds, 'if the ball hadn't stopped in the net, it would have continued in the air, drawing an incredible, repeating spiral trajectory.'

'I don't believe that we will ever see something quite like that again,' Fontanari said.

Israeli scientist Erez Garty also theorised about Roberto Carlos' kick. He gave a lesson for '*physics dummies*' on *YouTube* which explained the magic.

As the ball appears to head wide, a cameraman next to the goal thinks it's going to hit him — he ducks.

In the end, football is more art than science.

XV – Community

'You've got to tell the world how to treat you. If the world tells you how you are going to be treated, you are in trouble.'
— *James Baldwin*

59 Giuliani

Prepare relentlessly: Lessons from a master

'All politics is local.'
– *Rudy Giuliani*

Before he went over to the 'dark side', and became *The Penguin*, Rudolph W. Giuliani was a spectacular success.

He had a stellar legal career. As the US Attorney for the Southern District of New York, he was a fierce combatant against organised crime. He was twice elected Mayor of New York, and made a huge contribution to the safety, well-being, affluence and confidence in the city. His leadership on 9/11 and during its aftermath was significant and widely praised.

Overall, in the years 1994 to 2001, crime fell by 57% in NYC. The implementation of extensive anti-gun initiatives took 90,000 illegal firearms off the street. Unemployment went down from 11% to 6%. Times Square was revitalised and cleaned up. Twenty three city taxes were reduced or eliminated. The city placed 200,000 welfare recipients into jobs, a tenfold increase from 1993. Before his tenure, only 69% of the parks were graded and certified as 'acceptably clean'. In 2001, 91% enjoyed that designation.

Organised crime was removed from trash collection and food distribution. This saved local businesses around $600m a year – equivalent to the largest tax cut in city history.

By 1986, Giuliani indicted eleven organised crime figures, including the heads of New York City's so-called 'Five Families'. Leaders of the Five Families voted in 1986 to issue a contract on Giuliani's life.

Broken Windows

In criminology, the broken windows theory states that visible signs of crime, anti-social behaviour and civil disorder create an urban environment that encourages further crime and disorder, including serious crimes. The theory suggests that policing methods that target minor crimes such as vandalism, loitering, public drinking, and fare evasion help to create an atmosphere of order and lawfulness.

The theory was introduced in 1982 by social scientists James Wilson and George Kelling. It was popularized by New York City police commissioner William Bratton and mayor Giuliani, whose policies were influenced by the theory.

Fix the broken windows. That way people see that you actually care. Invest in neighbourhoods. That's why I've never understood why people oppose *gentrification*. I for one, don't want to get stabbed.

Giuliani was laser-like in his execution of this. By fixing the broken windows, this elevates overall behaviour. Look after the little details and the little problems, so that the big ones don't arise.

9/11

One reason why the city was quick to respond to the terrorist attacks on 9/11, was that they already had several different disaster recovery plans in place, and had trained for them. Not for an event of that scale, of course, but they had micro-plans for each agency – fire service, police, emergency response – so that they didn't have to start from nothing.

Giuliani outlined his approach to this relentless planning: 'We'd blueprint what each person in each agency would do if the city faced, say, a chemical attack or biomedical attack. We went through how we'd act in the event of a plane crash or a terrorist attack on a political gathering. We didn't just choreograph our response on paper, but we did trial runs on the streets, to test how long the plans took in practice.

We did not anticipate that airliners would be commandeered and turned into guided missiles, but the fact that we'd practiced for other kinds of disasters made us far more prepared to handle a catastrophe that nobody had envisioned.

The more planning we did, the more we would be ready for surprises. Before September 11, there were those who said we were being overly concerned. We didn't hear that afterward.'

23rd June 2022

Milton Keynes UK
Ingram Content Group UK Ltd.
UKHW010744180923
428890UK00001B/14

9 781915 996480

Marx, Karl 13, 164, 170-171, 210
Miller, Henry 94
More, Sir Thomas 28-31
Morrissey 18-20, 64, 67-69
Moses 65, 196
Murdoch, Iris 13
Murray, Douglas 219-220, 236
Music 18, 20, 22, 33-34, 63-69, 71, 75, 86-87, 196, 209-210, 226, 235
New York City 21-23, 107, 200, 216-218
Nixon, Richard 81, 84, 86
Obama, Barack 57, 171
The Odyssey 25
Oedipus 90-91
Olympic Games 57
Orwell, George 40, 103, 107, 131-133
Peterson, Jordan 60-62, 236
Pinter, Harold 129
Proust, Marcel 137
Reagan, Ronald 166
Rushdie, Sir Salman 39-40, 128-130, 189

Sartre, Jean-Paul 13, 42, 44, 232
Scruton, Sir Roger 13, 209-210, 219-221
Shakespeare 9, 28, 31, 81, 90, 92, 196, 210
The Smiths 19-20, 64, 66, 68, 70, 92
Sophocles 13, 49, 89-91
South Korea 138, 212
Stalin, Josef 14, 44, 79, 131-132
Steiner, George 209-211
Stoicism 52-54
Vietnam 139
Weil, Simone 12-17

Index

Antigone 89-91
Allen, Woody 233
Amis, Martin 40
Arendt, Hannah 152-157, 236
Aurelius, Marcus 52
Ayer, A.J. 25-27
Baldwin, James 215
Bierce, Ambrose 63, 127
Birmingham 60
de Beauvoir, Simone 13, 15
British Museum 61
Burgess, Anthony 163
Camus, Albert 12-13, 42-45, 206-208, 235
Churchill, Winston 83
Cyprus 60, 144-146
Delaney, Shelagh 18-20
Eichmann, Adolf 149-157, 236
Elizabeth, HM Queen 11, 33
Elvis 86-88
Friedman, Milton 107
Gallagher, Noel 66, 70, 72-73, 188

Gandhi, Mohandas 57, 75-78, 80, 196-197, 222-225, 236
de Gaulle, Charles 13
The Great Gatsby 57, 86
Greece 22, 53, 91, 182-183, 185-187
Greer, Germaine 209-211
Harris, Sam 236
Harvard University 99, 124, 235, 237
Hitchens, Christopher 39-41, 128
Homer 13, 25, 76
India 22, 75-77, 222-224
Japan 138, 177-180, 212
Jaws, film 56, 80
Kazantzakis, Nikos 162
King, Martin Luther 103, 195-197
Kissinger, Henry 40
Klopp, Jurgen 203-205
London 9, 18, 26, 28, 39, 57, 60, 84-85, 126, 176, 182, 201, 223, 225-226, 228, 236
Liverpool 203, 205, 211
Mandela, Nelson 9, 57

Wider references

Financial Times, The Times, i–Paper, The New York Times, London Review of Books, The New York Review of Books, The Economist, Harvard Business Review, A Dictionary of Classical Greek Quotations, edited by Marinos Yeroulanos, *The Spectator, Prospect, Tribune, Wired, Parikiaki, Reuters, The Telegraph, The New Yorker, Bloomberg, NPR, Institute of Economic Affairs, The Washington Post, The Rest is Politics podcast, Lex Fridman podcast, Substack, TK News by Matt Taibbi, The Marginalian.* Any articles in this book that have no date are previously unpublished.

Any copyright infringement is unintended. Every endeavour has been made to cite relevant sources. Any plagiarism in this book is inadvertent, and the result of sloth. All remaining errors are the author's.

The publishers will rectify any misappropriation or any unattributed sources.

41. *Eichmann in Jerusalem,* by Hannah Arendt
42. Camilla Cavendish, *Financial Times*
45. Howard Jacobson, *A Point of View*, BBC Radio 4, 07-10-22; Gary Stevenson and Mark Littlehouse debate, *Institute of Economic Affairs*
44. 'The Church in Poland and Its Political Influence', Suzanne Herby
46. *Power and the Idealists,* by Paul Berman; and *Dublin debate*: Sam Harris, Jordan Peterson, Douglas Murray, 2018
48. *The Subtle Art of Not Giving a Fuck,* by Mark Manson
52. Tom Kington in *The Times*; Angelo Amante at *Reuters*
53. Nancy Duarte
54. Further reading: Stafford, J., 'Part of town as an independent factor: the NORTH-FORCE merger in Manchester'. Cambridge University Press, 2023.
55. Geir Jordet, *Professor of Sports Science;* and Panikos Papagapiou
56. Copyright, *ESPN*. Additional research and contributions by Christiaan Pieter Lok, Darrin Johnson and Jonito Douwes Dekker.
59. *Leadership,* by Rudolph Giuliani
61. Irina Spector-Marks, 'Mr. Gandhi Visits Lancashire: A Study in Imperial Miscommunication', 2008, *Macalester College*
62. *Blue Labour*, by Maurice Glasman; *All In*, by Lisa Nandy

References

Sources and citations, by chapter

1. Peter Terrence; *In Our Time, BBC Radio 4*
2. Christy Wampoleis, Professor of French, *Princeton University*
4. Will Pavia, *The Times*
9. Copyright, *Charlie Rose LLC.*
10. *'Albert Camus: A Life'*, by Oliver Todd; Peter Lennon, in *The Guardian*
11. Charles Bremner, *The Times*
13. Donald Robertson, cognitive psychotherapist, author of *How to Think Like a Roman Emperor*.
16. Professor James Crossley, *'Biblical and Religious Language in the Manchester Music Scene, 1976-1994.'* Department of Biblical Studies, *University of Sheffield*
18. Johnny Marr interview with *Channel Bee*, 2009
25. Anjli Raval, *Financial Times*
26. Diana Brazzel
27. *'The Science Behind an Answer — How Watson Works'*, *IBM* video, *YouTube.*
29. *Harvard Business Review*
32. *Red Cobalt*, by Siddharth Kara; *The Joe Rogan Experience* #1912, 22-Dec-2022
36. Crisp, V. *'Cultural and societal factors in high-performing jurisdictions'*. Zhao, Y. *'Two decades of havoc: A synthesis of criticism against PISA'*, *Journal of Educational Change*
37. *No End in Sight,* directed by Charles Ferguson, 2007

Acknowledgements

Thank you to my family, relatives, friends and work colleagues past and present. Thank you to *The Jewish Chronicle* for kind permission to use the cover photograph *'Raw Materials: Textiles'* from the family archives of Sam Stockman.

Epilogue

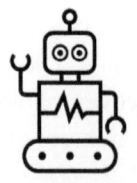

In the film *Sleeper*, written and directed by Woody Allen, modern day Miles Monroe wakes up to find that he is in the year 2173.

In an unfamiliar world, he nevertheless finds that much is the same.

He is taken to get measured up for some clothes at the Jewish robot tailors *Cohen & Ginsberg* ('Established 2073').

Chaperone: Anybody here? I have a new citizen to be outfitted.

Ginsberg (a robot tailor): What do you want, jackets? We got jackets. You want trousers? We got trousers. This is a good time, believe me. We're having a big sale. Tremendous. Positively the lowest prices. Maybe you need a nice double-knit. Incidentally, I'm stuck with three pieces corduroy.

Miles: Er, something simple.

Ginsberg: We got simple, we got complicated. What are you worrying?

– Sleeper (1973)

cockpit – a gesture of respect for the fortitude of a veteran Free French soldier.

(2) No plan survives contact with the 'enemy'.

You may have things mapped out, but life will change, so you need to adapt, and keep moving forward. Learn to improvise, and to make the most of unfamiliar situations. In Jean-Paul Sartre's lovely quip: 'In football, everything is complicated by the presence of the opposite team.'

(3) Ten minutes before.

Always be on time. Be there a few minutes before. You are part of something bigger, so if you are not where you're meant to be, others will suffer. Plan ahead.

(4) Go big, or go home.

Half–hearted effort is pointless. Always give everything. Start from where you are. The Army has an equivalent phrase: 'Be 10% braver'.

(5) Think to the finish.

Think of the end goals. How can you get there? What obstacles need to be overcome? Diamonds only form when extreme pressure is exerted on carbon.

31st March 2023

One hijacker kept a gun against the captain's head. 'Every time I tried to look in a different direction, he pressed the barrel of his gun against my neck,' Captain Bacos recalled.

Bacos was 52 years old. He had fought against Germany in World War II, having joined the Free French forces.

The jet refuelled in Libya. The hijackers then directed Bacos to fly to Entebbe Airport, in Idi Amin's Uganda.

The terrorists demanded $5 million and the release of dozens of Palestinian and pro-Palestinian militants imprisoned in Israel and other countries. They that said if their demands were not met, they would start to kill the hostages.

The hijackers then began to separate the Israeli and Jewish passengers from all others. It was an order reminiscent of the grisly process of selection in the Nazi camps.

'I fought the Nazis,' the captain said. 'I knew precisely what fascism was all about. The genocide is a horror that none of us had forgotten.' He tried to look after all his passengers, now hostages, in an empty air terminal.

The terrorists declared that those hostages who were not Jews could leave, and fly on to Paris.

Captain Bacos and his crew were invited to leave with them, but as he later told the BBC, 'I told my crew that we must stay until the end, because that was our tradition, so we cannot accept being freed. All my crew agreed without exception.'

Israeli commandos landed on July 4, 1976, in what became known as *Operation Entebbe*. Three hostages were killed during the raid, but 102 were rescued. On the flight back to Israel, the commandos invited Captain Bacos into the

63 Rules

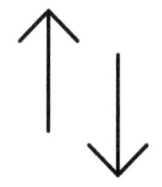

Five Rules for Life: A guide for all ages

'We hold these truths to be self-evident'
– *Thomas Jefferson,* 1776

(1) Leaders eat last.

Also known as *servant leadership*. Leaders protect their teams from above and make sure their troops are supported to be successful in their roles. This means allowing your team to shine and take the glory for their work. You're an enabler.

A great, and an extreme, example of this was the airline pilot, Michel Bacos. He was the captain of *Air France* Flight 139 on June 27, 1976, with more than 240 passengers and 12 crew, when it took off from Tel Aviv for Paris, with a stop in Athens.

About eight minutes after take-off from Athens, the plane was hijacked by terrorists from the *Popular Front for the Liberation of Palestine*, and the *Baader-Meinhof Gang*, a radical German group.

The lesson of *Northern Rock's* long success, is that institutions which are rooted in their communities, and where people have a stake in the success of that institution, can do incredible things.

A decade after its collapse, there are calls to recreate its role through regional investment banks or decentralised citizen's wealth funds, to spread prosperity and to create opportunity more widely.

9th March 2023

greatest degree of capital constraint in banking, just happens to generate the greatest value and is the most competitive.

Plus, it welcomed, absorbed, and 'levelled-up' that hungry, alcoholic, drug-addicted pauper that was known as East Germany, from 1989 onwards.

And yet. One glimpses this in England.

Geordies

Northern Rock was a building society that was built by the people of the North East to *serve* the people of the North East. It was central to the UK economy for many decades – with the region's mines, dockyards and shipyards.

It was a trusted institution – supporting home ownership and business growth.

In 1997 it demutualised and floated on the London Stock Exchange. It was exposed in the financial crash; and by 2007, it collapsed.

Nationalised by a Labour Government and sold off by the ensuing Coalition Government, its loss was a consequence of the short-term gains engineered for a few insiders.

Northern Rock saw its region through tough times and good for 150 years, weathering four major recessions. It provided hope to striking miners and their families when it suspended mortgage payments during the tough times of the 1980s.

When it collapsed, its sponsorship of *Newcastle United F.C.* was replaced by *Wonga*, a company that lends at 5,800% rates.

Market

In general, free markets tend to work well – the price mechanism, individual choice, the profit motive, productivity, eliminating inefficiency.

There is suspicion, however, of the globalised form of the free market. That it has lost the essence of local meaning and local forms of value, and has created inequalities.

Freedom of association led to the emergence of trade unions, insurance mutuals and friendly societies. The flourishing of these associations, from football clubs to professions, became a central feature of British life from the nineteenth-century onwards.

But now, these have become unrecognisable – 'corporatised' and remote. Mercurian cunning seemed to have trumped the Apollonian municipal impulse.

This isn't the case in Europe, however.

Civic

Germany has a vocational economy whereby self-organised institutions preserve and renew the traditions of a particular craft and regulate labour market entry. For example, regional banks are constrained to lend *within their region*. Also, there is significant representation of the workforce in the management and decision making of firms, in the form of *Worker Councils*.

The paradox of Europe is that the country with the greatest degree of labour voice in its corporations, the most intense system of vocational interference in labour markets, the

62 Grounded

A model for 'Levelling Up'

Among the Roman gods, Apollo and Mercury represented two types of people.

Apollo was rooted in place and epitomised stability, honour, agriculture and war.

Mercury was swift, mobile and delighted in trickery, music and literature.

For Apollonians, the Mercurians were cunning, lacking in courage, while valuing money and success over reliability and faithfulness. The Mercurians considered the Apollonians slow, stupid and provincial.

Both groups co-existed in society – Apollonians dominating the countryside and Mercurians flourishing in cities.

In Britain, this creative friction exists between urban and rural, between London and the provinces. Both forms of life – settled and transient, durable and fleeting, productive and commercial, crafts and arts – need each other for a flourishing civility.

Politics is a negotiation between these groups: the tension between tradition and modernity, conservatism and radicalism, continuity and change.

William Shirer, was a journalist at the Chicago Tribune. He was later to write the definitive book on the Third Reich. He wrote the following in 1931:—

'In London, Gandhi was the butt of jokes in the newspapers — a funny-looking man with the audacity to make demands of the British empire. By comparison, the industrial north, hardworking and not caring much about politics, received him differently. Lancashire liked him. Cotton magnates sat at his feet and listened to him.

They argued. They questioned. And they cheered: 'Three cheers for Mr Gandheye, hip, hip...' '

26th January 2023

Gandhi, while sympathetic to Lancashire's troubles, saw the visit as an opportunity to educate Lancashire on the nature of Indian nationalism, not to rescue the unemployed textile workers. He told them the boycott was not the main cause of their downturn, and that the boycott was a social and spiritual necessity for Indians.

Two worlds

Gandhi's visit to England had little to do with the Round Table Conference, and rather more to do with exposing the British people to his ideals of Indian nationalism. Gandhi did not trust 'the unbending Government' to provide any changes to India's status.

In an article entitled '*What I Want*' published in *The Evening Standard*, Gandhi stated, 'I want peace for India. I want the people of Britain to help me.'

Gandhi and the Lancashire mill workers had such different visions of the past and the future that they could not communicate effectively about the causes and solutions to the boycott. The cotton industry romanticised Lancashire's economic past, and they interpreted the Indian boycott as a momentary hiccup in normal business.

It took nearly 20 years and another world war before India achieved self-rule. By that time the Lancashire textile industry was in steady decline.

Some of the weavers told him how bad things were on his visit to Darwen. He replied: 'My dear, you have no idea what poverty is.'

Gandhi was 62, and in London for the Round Table Conference on India's future.

Gandhi encouraged Indians to boycott British goods and buy Indian goods instead. This helped to revitalise local economies in India and it also hit the British economy.

Gandhi's sympathies lay with the workers, not the textile manufacturers. He said: 'They treated me as one of their own. I shall never forget that.'

Dialogue

Gandhi met mill workers and mill owners and civic dignitaries. He looked around at the smart houses of Garden Village which the Davies family had built for the workers, and he couldn't quite square it all with the poverty of his own country.

The boycott would stay unless there was progress towards independence, he told them.

The Lancashire textile industry had been in a depression for ten years. The Indian boycott, though only one factor, and not a very important one, in Lancashire's decline, was targeted by industrialists and trade unionists as the cause of the trade depression. At the same time, Indian nationalists blamed Lancashire for the suppression of the Indian textile industry. Yet Gandhi and the Lancashire mill owners and workers engaged in 'frank, friendly discussion'.

One day he was able to teach the children in the neighbourhood about *ahimsa* (non-violence) and about the common roots between Sanskrit and English words.

61 Lancashire

Gandhi's Lancashire: cotton mills and independence

'A crowd numbering three thousand assembled at Darwen station. But hopes were quickly dashed when the first passenger to see the crowd shouted, *'You can all go home. He got off at Springvale station.'*
– *The Darwen News,* 26 September, 1931

Arrival

Darwen and Springvale were economically depressed cotton towns in Lancashire. 'He' was Mohandas Gandhi, leader of the Indian National Congress, whose boycott of English cotton goods was at its height.

Gandhi visited Lancashire in 1931 after accepting an invitation from the mill-owning Davies family. They wanted him to see the hardship suffered by the Lancashire textile industry, which had been affected by the Indian independence movement's boycott of British goods.

The Davies family were prominent Socialists and Quakers, and they firmly believed that Gandhi might understand the suffering throughout the mill towns such as Bolton, Oldham, Burnley and Blackburn.

way. But the legacy of thinking and feeling and of moral being is still there with us, and it's been inherited by all our institutions – the law courts, Parliament, local authority council chambers, museums, ministries of state, the health service, libraries, the emergency services, universities, the Charity Commission, the Supreme Court. And the attempt to dispense with it does hollow out those institutions – it leaves them spiritually vacant.

It's up to people of faith, to try and fill them again. And you can only do that from your own heart, you can't do that by asking anyone else to impose it for you. Christians are called to do this. And the more Christians there are, the more likely it is that it will happen.

One shouldn't despair. We're in the same situation as the Christians in the catacombs, and we have to keep the light burning down there.

12th January, 2023

60 Light

Belonging and community: Left v. Right

Extracted and adapted from The Spectator: Live Event, 8 May 2019, with Roger Scruton and Douglas Murray

Roger Scruton: You can't defend communities simply by letting the market loose upon them. You travel around France, and you visit these beautiful towns and villages. And you ask yourself the question, 'How wonderful that these things exist, how did it happen?' It didn't happen just because people build like that, it happened because people believed in the place they were building in, and also believed in controlling each other to make sure that individuals didn't spoil those places.

Politically, if you are in the business of repudiating things, of throwing things away, declaring your emancipation from your past, you get an audience pretty quickly. And you easily find things to say. But, if you are trying to defend your sense of belonging in this world, words quickly run out.

The Left has always been good at slogans: 'March!' 'Forward', and 'Into the Future'.

If you think what a slogan would be on the conservative side, it would be something like 'Hesitate!' It just doesn't work.

Douglas Murray: I once saw an example of that. One of the only protests I've turned up to, at some point we all chanted something and then we stopped. We did it once and I said to one of the friends: 'We're not very good at this, are we?' And she said: 'Well, our view Douglas is, if we've said something once, that's quite enough'. And that's a difference of habit. I don't want to keep on saying the same thing.

RS: It goes to the heart of what we think communication is. If you think of communication as an exercise in respect for the other, then you don't repeat yourself. Repeating yourself suggests that you're either demented or that you just don't care about the other person's response; you're prepared to override it and say the same thing again and again. There's no way in which a chanted slogan invites an answer. I think there's a whole politics of that kind which grows out of the mass movements on the Left but also invades the language of the Left.

Audience member: The great slogans for conservatism are probably to be found in the New Testament. Do you think that conservatism, or enlightened classical liberalism, is fatally wounded without Christianity?

DM: Wow. Very good question.

RS: We have inherited from the Enlightenment of the 18th century – that flowering of science and reason and the withdrawal from superstition – the idea that religion is essentially a private affair.

Even if we do have this formal, official religion in this country, it is not imposed on us in any particularly emphatic